FCE Result

Student's Book

Paul A Davies & Tim Falla

OXFORD

UNIVERSITY PRESS

Contents

Lead in at the start of every unit	**Review** at the end of every unit	**Exam Overview** page 4

Listening	Speaking	Use of English	Vocabulary	Writing
Part 4 Multiple choice	Part 1	Part 4 Key word transformations	Using a dictionary	Part 2 An informal letter
Part 2 Sentence completion	Part 2	Part 2 Open cloze	Collective nouns	Part 1 A formal email
Part 1 Multiple choice	Parts 3 and 4	Part 1 Multiple-choice cloze	Phrasal verbs with *put*	Part 2 A story
Part 1 Multiple choice	Part 2	Part 2 Open cloze	Phrasal verbs with *take*	Part 2 A review
Part 4 Multiple choice	Part 1	Part 3 Word formation	Idioms connected with speech	Part 2 An essay
Part 1 Multiple choice	Part 3	Part 4 Key word transformations	Idioms with *come* and *go*	Part 1 An informal email
Part 3 Multiple matching	Parts 3 and 4	Part 1 Multiple-choice cloze	Phrasal verbs	Part 1 An informal email
Part 3 Multiple matching	Parts 3 and 4	Part 3 Word formation	Word pairs	Part 2 A report
Part 2 Sentence completion	Part 2	Part 4 Key word transformations	Body idioms	Part 1 A letter
Part 3 Multiple matching	Part 2	Part 3 Word formation	Expressions with *mind*	Part 1 A letter
Part 4 Multiple choice	Parts 3 and 4	Part 2 Open cloze	Compound nouns	Part 1 A letter of complaint
Part 2 Sentence completion	Part 2	Part 1 Multiple-choice cloze	Compound adjectives	Part 2 An article

Exam Overview

Introduction

The First Certificate of English corresponds to Level Three in the Cambridge ESOL five-level system. It also corresponds to the Association of Language Teachers in Europe (ALTE) Level Three, and Council of Europe level B2.

There are five papers in the examination, each worth 20% of the total marks. To achieve a passing grade (A, B or C) candidates must achieve approximately 60% of the total marks available, or above. Candidates' grades are based on the total score from all five papers and there is no pass or fail grade for individual papers.

Paper 1 Reading (1 hour)

This paper has three parts, each with a text or texts and comprehension questions. There are 30 questions in total.

The texts may consist of several short pieces, and the length of each text may be between 550–700 words.

The texts are taken from newspapers, magazines, reports, fiction, advertisements, leaflets, brochures, etc.

Part	Number of items	What you do	What it tests	How to do it
1	8	Choose the best answer from four option multiple-choice questions.	Your understanding of a text and opinions expressed in it.	page 10
2	7	Decide where sentences belong in a text.	Your understanding of text structure and development.	page 94
3	15	Match prompts from a list to elements in a text.	Your ability to find specific information.	page 22

Marks

One mark for each correct answer to the multiple-matching tasks.

Two marks for each correct answer to the multiple-choice and gapped text tasks.

Paper 2 Writing (1 hour 20 minutes)

This paper has two parts. The Part 1 question is a compulsory letter or email, and is based on input information. In Part 2 you choose one question from four; Question 5 has two options on a set reading text.

Answers for Part 1 should be 120–150 words in length, and for Part 2 120–180 words.

The task types for Part 2 will be from the following: article, essay, letter, report, review, story.

Examples of Paper 2 question types can be found in the Writing Guide on pages 155–163.

Part	Task type	Number of items	What you do	What it tests	How to do it
1	Compulsory contextualised task based on input material of up to 160 words, which could be from advertisements, extracts from letters, emails, etc.	One compulsory task.	Write according to the task instructions.	Your ability to process input material and select and apply it according to the instructions.	page 79
2	Contextualised task in no more than 70 words.	One from a choice of four questions; Question 5 has two options.		Your ability to write according to the instructions, in the correct style, layout and register in order to have a positive effect on the reader.	page 19 page 55

Marks

Parts 1 and 2 have equal marks.

Paper 3 Use of English (45 minutes)

This paper has four parts, and a total of 42 questions.

The testing focus is on understanding and controlling formal elements of language (e.g. grammar, word formation, spelling).

Part	Task type	Number of items	What you do	What it tests	How to do it
1	Multiple-choice cloze	12	Fill 12 gaps in a text choosing from four-option multiple-choice items.	Phrases, collocations, idioms, phrasal verbs, linkers, used to complete a text with the correct meaning and grammatical context.	page 89
2	Open cloze	12	Fill 12 gaps in a text with one word per gap.	Your awareness and control of structural items.	page 28
3	Word formation	10	Form appropriate words from prompts to complete 10 gaps in a text.	Word formation.	page 64
4	Key word transformations	8	Complete a gapped sentence with two to five words, including a key word, so that it has the same meaning as the lead-in sentence.	Your awareness and control of grammatical and lexical items.	page 112

Marks

Parts 1, 2 and 3: one mark for each correct answer.

Part 4: each answer receives up to 2 marks.

Paper 4 Listening (approx. 40 minutes)

This paper has four parts, and 30 questions.

The recorded texts may include the following:

Monologues: announcements, radio broadcasts, telephone messages, speeches, talks, lectures, etc.

Conversations between two or three speakers: conversations, interviews, discussions.

The testing focus is on understanding specific information, gist, attitude, opinion, main points and detail.

All parts are heard twice. The instructions are given on the question paper and are also heard. The recordings include a variety of voices, styles of delivery and accents.

Part	Task type	Number of items	What you do	What it tests	How to do it
1	Multiple choice	8	Listen to eight unrelated extracts and choose the best answer from three-option multiple-choice items.	Your understanding of gist, detail, function, purpose, attitude, situation, genre, etc.	page 50
2	Sentence completion	10	Listen to a monologue or text involving interacting speakers and complete gaps in sentences with information from the text.	Your understanding of detail, specific information, stated opinion.	page 110
3	Multiple matching	5	Listen to five short related monologues and select the correct option from a list of six.	As Part 1.	page 98
4	Multiple choice	7	Listen to a monologue or text involving interacting speakers and choose the best answer from three-option multiple-choice items.	Your understanding of opinion, attitude, gist, main idea, specific information.	page 14

Marks

One mark for each correct answer.

Spelling must be correct for common words and those considered easy to spell.

Paper 5 Speaking (approx. 14 minutes)

This paper has four parts.

The standard format is two candidates and two examiners, one acting as interlocutor and assessor, the other acting as assessor only. In certain circumstances, three candidates may sit the test together.

Part	Task type	Length	What you do	What it tests	How to do it
1	A conversation between the interlocutor and each candidate.	3 minutes	Ask and answer 'personal' questions.	Your ability to use general interactional and social language.	page 15
2	Individual long turns and brief responses.	1 minute long turn for each candidate and 20-second response from the second candidate.	Talk about visual prompts.	Your ability to describe, compare, express opinions.	page 123
3	Two-way interaction between candidates.	3 minutes	Discuss a problem-solving task based on visual and/or written prompts.	Your ability to exchange ideas, express and justify opinions, agree and disagree, speculate, reach a decision through negotiation, etc.	page 39
4	A discussion between candidates and the interlocutor.	4 minutes	Discuss issues related to the Part 3 topic.	Your ability to express and justify opinions, agree and/or disagree.	page 86

Marks

Candidates are assessed on their performance throughout the test in the following areas:

• Grammar and vocabulary (accuracy and appropriacy)

• Discourse management (ability to express ideas in coherent, connected speech)

• Pronunciation (individual sounds, linking of words, stress and intonation)

• Interactive communication (turn-taking, initiating and responding)

• Global achievement (overall effectiveness in the tasks)

The assessor marks according to detailed Analytical Scales, the interlocutor gives a mark on a Global Scale, which is less detailed.

The circle of life

Lead in

1 Name any of the people you recognise in the photos. Guess who is related and what the relationships are.

2 Compare your answers to 1 in pairs. Say which physical features a–g helped you to guess.

   a skin tone (fair/dark/tanned)
   b hair colour (black/fair/blond/red)
   c hairstyle (curly/straight)
   d eye colour (blue/green/hazel/brown)
   e eyebrows (bushy/thin)
   f nose (large/small/hooked/turned up)
   g mouth (full/thin lips)

3 Turn to page 153 to find out the answers to 1.

4 Work in pairs. Find out from your partner whether
- they look like one or both parents.
- they look like another relative in some way.
- they have a similar personality to a parent or sibling (brother or sister).

Reading

Part 1 Multiple choice

1 Would you like to have an identical twin? What advantages and disadvantages might there be?

2 Read the text opposite quickly. Do cases like the 'Jim twins' tell scientists a, b or c?

   a why some women give birth to identical twins

   b which physical features we inherit from which parent

   c how much of our personality we inherit from our parents

how to do it

- Read the text quickly for general meaning.
- Read the questions first. Don't read the options (A–D) yet.
- Underline the parts of the text that contain the information you need.
- Read the options and look again at the relevant part of the text. Cross out any options that are clearly wrong.
- If you can't decide between two options, make an intelligent guess.

3 Read the **how to do it** box. Then read the text again carefully, and for questions 1–8, choose the answer (A, B, C or D) which you think fits best, according to the text.

  1 Identical twins look the same

    A but usually have very different characters.

    B and are usually identical in character too.

    C and are often very similar in character too.

    D but rarely think in the same way.

  2 Unlike non-identical twins, identical twins are

    A more common among Asians than Africans.

    B becoming more and more common.

    C more common among older mothers.

    D equally common everywhere.

  3 Scientists are particularly interested in identical twins who

    A have been raised by different families.

    B are genetically exactly the same.

    C look and behave in very similar ways.

    D are not alike in terms of personality.

  4 While they were growing up, twins Jim Lewis and Jim Springer

    A were in regular contact.

    B knew about their twin, but had no contact.

    C did not know they had ever had a twin.

    D were prevented from seeing each other by their adoptive families.

  5 When the two Jims met as adults, how did they react to the similarities between them?

    A They had always expected them.

    B They found them very amusing.

    C They did not realise how similar they were until the researchers told them.

    D They were very surprised.

  6 As adults, the twins

    A both had only one child.

    B both got married twice.

    C had pets with the same name.

    D married women who were identical twins.

  7 How do other cases of twins raised apart compare with the 'Jim twins'?

    A They are all just as surprising.

    B They are less surprising, but often show interesting coincidences.

    C Many of them are even more surprising.

    D Most of them show that other pairs of identical twins are not very similar.

  8 According to the text, you might find it difficult to change your personality because

    A only other people can change it.

    B it is determined mainly by how your parents treat you.

    C you can't control your surroundings.

    D you get your personality from your parents.

THE JIM TWINS

You take it for granted that you are a unique person, different from everybody else on Earth, and you understand that everybody else is also unique. Identical twins are fascinating because they
5 challenge this notion: they are unique people, of course, but they're also unnervingly similar to each other – and not only in terms of appearance. They often share opinions, mannerisms and personality traits.

Identical twins are rare, occurring in
10 about three out of every 1,000 births. They seem to occur at random, regardless of the age or ethnic background of the mother (unlike non-identical twins which are, for
15 example, far more common among Africans than Asians). Although there may be tiny differences in physical appearances between two identical twins, which allow family and close
20 friends to tell them apart, they do have exactly the same DNA. This is because they develop from a single 'egg which divides in two during the very early stages of pregnancy.

25 For scientists, the non-physical similarities between identical twins are the most interesting: are they the result of growing up together in the same home, or are they the result of their identical DNA? By
30 studying identical twins who have not grown up together, researchers can see which similarities remain and which disappear. In other words, they can learn which aspects of a person's identity are determined by genes and which are influenced by the environment. The Minnesota Twin
35 Study is probably the best-known twin study to date. The study provides information about how our environment and genes work together to influence everything from attitudes, talents and abilities, to job selection, to falling in love, to aging and health.

40 Identical twins Jim Lewis and Jim Springer were only four weeks old when they were separated; each infant was taken in by a different adoptive family. At age five, Lewis learned that he had a twin, but he said that the idea never truly 'soaked in' until he was 38 years old.
45 Springer learned of his twin at age eight, but both he and his adoptive parents believed the brother had died. The two Jims were finally reunited at age 39.

The similarities the twins shared not only amazed one another, but also amazed researchers at the University of
50 Minnesota. The very fact that both twins were given the same name was a big coincidence. But there's more.

- As youngsters, each Jim had a dog named 'Toy'.
- Each Jim had been married twice – the first wives were both called Linda and the second wives were
55 both called Betty.
- One Jim had named his son James Allan and the other Jim had named his son James Alan.
- Each twin had driven his light-blue Chevrolet to the same beach in Florida for family vacations.
60 - Both Jims had at one time held part-time posts as sheriffs.
- Both were fingernail biters and suffered from migraine headaches.

While not as eerily similar as the Jim twins, many more
65 instances of strange likenesses can be found among twins who were raised apart. For example, identical twins Tom Patterson and Steve Tazumi had very different upbringings. Raised in a Christian family by two janitors in rural Kansas, Tom still managed to choose the same
70 career as his brother. Steve, who lives in Philadelphia, was raised in a Buddhist household. Both men own body-building gyms.

It's obvious from these twins' stories that genetics are a major factor in shaping who we are. In fact, research so
75 far indicates that characteristics such as personality are mainly related to genes. This means that our character traits as adults are largely determined before we are born – and there is very little that we, or anybody else, can do to change them.

4 Discuss your reaction to the final sentence in the text, giving reasons. Do you believe it, and if so, do you think it is a good or bad thing?

Vocabulary

Describing personality

1 In pairs, discuss whether the personality adjectives in the box below are

a good

b bad

c either good or bad

> argumentative   arrogant   bossy   easy-going
> eccentric   honest   loyal   narrow-minded
> open-minded   sensible   sensitive

2 ◗ Listen to five people describing a friend or relative. Choose the best adjective from 1 to sum up their description.

Speaker 1 thinks that her uncle is ....

Speaker 2 thinks that his brother is ....

Speaker 3 thinks that her friend is ....

Speaker 4 thinks that his cousin is ....

Speaker 5 thinks that her father is ....

3 Read the **tip** box then think of three people you know well and describe them to a partner. Use adjectives from 1 and give examples of their behaviour.

Example   My sister, Belinda, is very sensible. For example, she always goes to bed early if she has a busy day the next day.

> **tip** You may be asked to describe somebody's character in Writing Part 2 or Speaking Part 1. When we use personality adjectives to describe somebody, we often use them with modifying adverbs like *very, a bit, rather, quite,* etc.

Grammar

Talking about the future GR p165

1 Choose the best verb form (a–c) to complete sentences 1–7.

1 By the time we get to the nightclub, most people .... home.

  a will go

  b are going

  c will have gone

2 The train to London .... at 6.13, so let's meet at the station at 6 o'clock.

  a is going to leave

  b leaves

  c is leaving

3 As soon as I save enough money, ... you a laptop.

  a I buy

  b I'll buy

  c I'll have bought

4 By the time she leaves music school, she .... the piano for 12 years.

  a will study

  b will be studying

  c will have been studying

5 Louis won't be at school tomorrow because .... in a swimming tournament.

  a he's taking part

  b he'll take part

  c he takes part

6 This time next month, we .... around Thailand.

  a will travel

  b are travelling

  c will be travelling

7 My sister doesn't feel well, so .... at home this afternoon.

  a she'll have stayed

  b she stays

  c she's going to stay

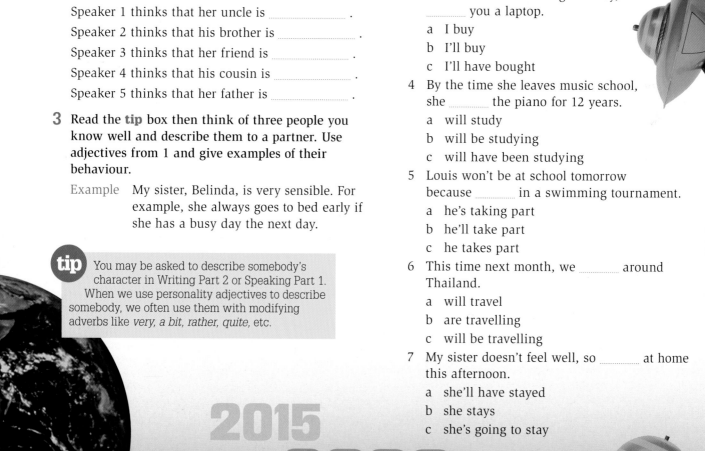

2015
2020
2025

2 Complete sentences a–g with the tenses below, and match them with the sentences in 1. Check your answers in the Grammar Reference.

> future continuous   future perfect simple
> future perfect continuous   *going to* future
> present continuous   present simple   *will* future

a We use the _____ to talk about things that we've arranged to do in the future.

b We use the _____ to talk about things that we've personally decided to do in the future.

c We use the _____ to make offers and promises and predictions.

d We use the _____ to talk about actions in progress in the future.

e We use the _____ to talk about completed actions in the future.

f We use the _____ to talk about future events that are part of a schedule or timetable.

g We use the _____ to say how long future actions will have been in progress.

3 Work in pairs. Tell your partner about something that

a humans can't do now but you think they'll be able to do by 2050.

b takes place next summer.

d exists today but will have disappeared by the year 2050, in your opinion.

e you're going to do as soon as you can afford it.

f you're doing next week.

4 Read the dialogue below. Underline any verb forms that you think are unnatural and replace them with better alternatives.

Martin Hi, is Jacqui there?

Lucy Yes, she is. Wait a moment, I'm just getting her.

Martin Thanks!

Jacqui Hi, it's Jacqui here.

Martin This is Martin. Listen carefully, I haven't got much time. Can you meet me at the port in one hour? The next boat to Tripoli will leave at 7:35.

Jacqui I can't! I'll have dinner with some people from work this evening. I've just arranged it.

Martin But we must leave tonight! By tomorrow, the newspapers are going to get hold of the story. We won't have been able to move without attracting attention.

Jacqui What story? Are you telling me what's going on?

Martin I explain everything as soon as we'll get to Tripoli. Trust me.

Jacqui Can't you explain now?

Martin There's no time. But if you don't do as I say, then by this time tomorrow, every journalist in town will knock at your door.

5 Read these predictions, ignoring the underlining. Say which ones you believe are true or false for you. Give reasons.

a <u>I don't think I'll ever</u> appear on television.

b <u>I reckon I'll</u> write a novel <u>one day</u>.

c <u>I don't imagine I'll</u> be earning much money in five years' time.

d <u>I guess</u> I'll be living in this town in ten years' time.

6 In pairs, talk about your ideas for your future using the questions below. Try to use some of the underlined phrases from 5 in your answers.

a Do you think you'll ever
  • experience space travel?
  • work abroad?
  • have a face-lift?
  • become a politician?
  • own a Ferrari?

b In five years' and 25 years' time, what kind of
  • house will you be living in?
  • clothes will you be wearing?
  • hobbies will you be doing?
  • holiday will you be going on?
  • job will you be doing?

Listening

Part 4 Multiple choice

1 Imagine that scientists could develop an 'immortality pill' that allowed people to live forever. Discuss these questions.

a   Would you take it? Why/Why not?

b   Would you want everyone to take it? Why/Why not?

 how to do it

You will have one minute to look at the questions. Read as much as you can in that time.

As you listen for the first time, mark the options that you think are correct.

Use the second listening to check your answers.

2 ◄)) You will hear an excerpt from a radio programme about living forever. Read the **how to do it** box, then listen and choose the best answers for 1–7.

1   According to some scientists, technology that allows people to live for thousands of years

   A   already exists.

   B   will definitely exist within 30 years.

   C   may exist within 30 years.

2   According to the speaker, why are scientists closer to finding this technology?

   A   They are beginning to understand why and how our bodies age.

   B   Medical technology is improving quickly.

   C   There are more old people in our societies.

3   According to some people, immortality would have a negative effect because

   A   we would soon use up all the earth's natural resources.

   B   everybody would stop caring about the environment.

   C   the earth would become very overcrowded.

4   What might people have to agree to do, before being allowed to live forever?

   A   suggest ways of dealing with over-population

   B   not have too many children

   C   not commit any serious crimes

5   If you were immortal, you might find it difficult to get up in the morning because

   A   you would be exhausted after thousands of other mornings.

   B   you would know there were going to be thousands more mornings.

   C   the technology that kept you alive might make you very weak.

6   Some people say that immortality would be pointless because

   A   only the very rich would be able to afford it.

   B   you wouldn't use your time carefully.

   C   you would only remember a part of your life.

7   You might never fall in love if you were immortal because

   A   the most powerful human feelings come from knowing that we will not be here forever.

   B   you would get bored with everybody that you've met.

   C   the technology would change the way in which your brain experiences emotions.

3 Discuss what age you would choose to be if you could stay the same age forever. Give reasons. Think about the following.

- appearance
- daily routine
- independence
- health
- wealth
- wisdom

Speaking

Part 1

1 Read questions a–f below, then match each one with a pair of words (1–6) that you might hear in the answer.

   a Do you enjoy spending time alone? (Why/Why not?)

   b What do you use the Internet for?

   c Tell me about a close friend.

   d Tell me about the most beautiful place you have ever visited.

   e Do you prefer physical or mental challenges?

   f What's your favourite TV programme and why?

   1 research   downloading

   2 scenery   spectacular

   3 dramas   plot

   4 share   solitary

   5 easy-going   loyal

   6 satisfying   achievement

2 Listen to six different students answering the questions in 1. Put questions a–f in the order that you hear the answers, using the words you matched them with to help you.

   1 ....   4 ....

   2 ....   5 ....

   3 ....   6 ....

3 Choose the correct word to complete these phrases from the listening in 2. Then say whether each phrase shows the end of an answer or a contrast.

   a … *from/in* my view, anyway.

   b That's my *opinion/thought*, anyway.

   c But on *another/the other* hand …

   d So, *at/in* short …

   e But at the *one/same* time, …

   f Although I must *admit/advise* that …

   g And that's about *it/that*, really.

   h Having said *it/that*, …

   i So all *for/in* all …

4 Write two questions on each of these topics.

   a future plans

   b family

   c daily routine

   d where you live

5 Read the **how to do it** box, and in pairs ask and answer questions from 1 and 4.

how to do it

Listen carefully to the question and try to repeat at least one of the key words in your reply.

Speak clearly and look at the person you are talking to.

Try to include some set phrases like the ones in 3.

Use of English

Part 4 Key word transformations

1 Read the **tip** box below, then match the underlined phrases in sentences a–f with 1–6.

a The USA did not <u>take part in</u> the 1980 Olympic Games in Moscow.

b When preparing for a hike, it's important to <u>take into account</u> what the weather will be like.

c At the age of one, a baby is just starting to <u>make sense of</u> the world around him.

d Marianne agreed to be home by midnight because she didn't want to <u>have a row</u> with her parents.

e It's arrogant to <u>make fun of</u> other people's achievements.

f Several factors <u>play a part in</u> the success or failure of a film.

1	argue	4	laugh at
2	consider	5	join in
3	be a cause of	6	understand

> **tip** Phrases like those underlined in 1 usually appear in dictionaries under the noun rather than the verb. You may have to read the entry carefully to find them.

2 Using a dictionary, find verbs to replace 1–6 in the text below.

Last weekend, I organised an 80th birthday party for my grandfather. Two of my brothers agreed to ¹<u>lend a hand</u> with the preparations. Our sister Rachel was out of the country at the time. My grandfather has so many grandchildren now, he sometimes ²<u>loses track of</u> their names, but Rachel has always been a favourite. I ³<u>let her know</u> about the party, and she ⁴<u>got in touch with</u> our grandfather on the day to ⁵<u>say sorry</u> for not being there. She ⁶<u>gave him her word</u> that she would visit him as soon as she returned home.

3 Rewrite each sentence a–f keeping the meaning the same. Use two to five words including the word given.

a Students at the summer school are expected to participate in leisure activities.
part
Students at the summer school are expected to .... leisure activities.

b Stubborn people often find it difficult to apologise for their mistakes.
sorry
Stubborn people often find it difficult .... their mistakes.

c Considering that my grandmother is so old, her memory is amazing.
account
If you .... old my grandmother is, her memory is amazing.

d Contacting a doctor on a Sunday can be difficult.
touch
It can be difficult to .... with a doctor on a Sunday.

e When he first moved to London, some of the children at school used to laugh at his accent.
make
When he first moved to London, some of the children at school used to .... his accent.

f When she invited us for dinner, we promised that we wouldn't be late.
word
When she invited us for dinner, we .... that we wouldn't be late.

Vocabulary

Using a dictionary

belt 0— /belt/ *noun, verb*
- *noun* **1** a long narrow piece of leather, cloth, etc. that you wear around the waist: *to **do up/fasten/tighten a belt*** ◊ *a belt buckle*—picture ⇨ PAGE R15—see also BLACK BELT, LIFEBELT, SEAT BELT, SUSPENDER BELT **2** a continuous band of material that moves round and is used to carry things along or to drive machinery—see also CONVEYOR BELT, FAN BELT **3** an area with particular characteristics or where a particular group of people live: *the country's **corn/industrial belt*** ◊ *We live in the **commuter belt**.* ◊ *a belt of rain moving across the country*—see also GREEN BELT **4** (*informal*) an act of hitting sth/sb hard: *She gave the ball a terrific belt.* **IDM** **below the 'belt** (of a remark) unfair or cruel: *That was distinctly below the belt!* ,**belt and 'braces** (*informal*) taking more actions than are really necessary to make sure that sth succeeds or works as it should: *a belt-and-braces policy* **have sth under your 'belt** (*informal*) to have already achieved or obtained sth: *She already has a couple of good wins under her belt.*—more at TIGHTEN
- *verb* **1** [VN] (*informal*) to hit sb/sth hard: *He belted the ball right out of the park.* ◊ *I'll belt you if you do that again.* **2** [V + *adv./prep.*] (*informal, especially BrE*) to move very fast **SYN** TEAR: *A truck came belting up behind us.* **3** [VN] to fasten a belt around sth: *The dress was belted at the waist.* **PHR V** ,**belt sth↔'out** (*informal*) to sing a song or play music loudly ,**belt 'up** (*BrE*) **1** (*NAmE* ,**buckle 'up**) (*informal*) to fasten your SEAT BELT (= a belt worn by a passenger in a vehicle) **2** (*informal*) used to tell sb rudely to be quiet **SYN** SHUT UP: *Just belt up, will you!*

pale 0— /peɪl/ *adj., verb, noun*
- *adj.* (**paler, pal·est**) **1** (of a person, their face, etc.) having skin that is almost white; having skin that is whiter than usual because of illness, a strong emotion, etc.: *a pale complexion* ◊ *pale with fear* ◊ *to **go/turn pale*** ◊ *You look pale. Are you OK?* ◊ *The ordeal left her looking **pale and drawn**.* **2** light in colour; containing a lot of white: *pale blue eyes* ◊ *a paler shade of green* ◊ *a pale sky* **OPP** DARK, DEEP **3** (of light) not strong or bright: *the cold pale light of dawn*—see also PALLID, PALLOR ▸ **pale·ly** /'peɪlli/ *adv.*: *Mark stared palely (= with a pale face) at his plate.* **pale·ness** *noun* [U]
- *verb* [V] ~ (**at sth**) to become paler than usual: *She (= her face) paled visibly at the sight of the police car.* ◊ *The blue of the sky paled to a light grey.* **IDM** '**pale beside/next to sth** | '**pale in/by comparison (with/to sth)** | '**pale into insignificance** to seem less important when compared with sth else: *Last year's riots pale in comparison with this latest outburst of violence.*
- *noun* **IDM** be,**yond the 'pale** considered by most people to be unacceptable or unreasonable: *His remarks were clearly beyond the pale.*

Oxford Advanced Learner's Dictionary, 7th edition

1 Read the two dictionary entries opposite. Find at least one example of a–h.

a a synonym (a word with the same meaning)

b an opposite

c an idiom

d a meaning which only exists in British English

e an American English equivalent

f an informal expression

g a phrasal verb

h an impolite expression

2 Match the underlined words in a–f with the relevant part of the dictionary entries. Give the part of speech and number.

a NASA is planning to send a probe to explore the asteroid <u>belt</u>.

b When Julie arrived home, she looked <u>pale</u> and worried.

c The <u>pale</u> winter sun provided little warmth.

d A police car came <u>belting</u> round the corner with its siren on.

e I don't think giving the TV a <u>belt</u> is going to make it work!

f Unusually, she has dark skin and <u>pale</u> blue eyes.

3 Rewrite sentences a–f replacing the underlined words with one of the dictionary entries opposite.

Example   When his car wouldn't start, he <u>hit</u> it.

When his car wouldn't start, he gave it a belt.

a Drivers and passengers should <u>fasten their seatbelts</u> even for short journeys.

b Just <u>shut up</u>! I can't hear myself think!

c His salary <u>is nothing</u> in comparison with the amount of money his wife earns.

d Some of the comedian's jokes were <u>completely unacceptable</u>.

e The van was <u>tearing along</u> the motorway at 140 kph.

f As the last song of the concert, the band <u>loudly performed</u> *America the Beautiful*.

Writing

Part 2 An informal letter

1 Read the end of Chloe's letter opposite and Megan's reply below it. Underline eight words which are too formal and think of less formal alternatives.

2 Read Megan's letter again and say which of these activities she is planning to do during the summer holidays.

a	buy some new clothes	e	hang out with friends
b	do nothing for a week	f	learn to surf
c	do some schoolwork	g	look for a job
d	go abroad	h	take exams

3 Divide the main part of Megan's letter into these four paragraphs.

a the immediate future
b a trip abroad
c getting a job
d questions for Chloe

4 Find a formal word in each of the sentences below and replace it with a less formal word.

a All I have to do is assist with the housework while I'm there.
b I've even informed my friends that I don't want to go out that week!
c You know, the one who resembles Penelope Cruz.
d I need to earn some funds before the next school year begins.

5 Match sentences a–d from 4 with each of the four paragraphs in Megan's letter.

Anyway, that's enough about me. What are your plans for the summer? Please write and tell me.

Best wishes

Chloe

Dear Chloe

I finish my end-of-year examinations on 14th June, and then I'm on holiday for eight weeks! I can't wait! I'll really need a good rest, therefore I'm going to spend the first week doing absolutely nothing! Later in the summer, I'll be visiting my uncle, who resides in Italy, for a couple of weeks. I haven't got sufficient money for the plane ticket, but luckily my uncle has offered to purchase it for me. He's so generous! He'll be working while I'm there, so I'll have his house (and swimming pool) to myself! As soon as I get back from Italy, I'm going to look for employment. My brother will have left his job at the leisure centre to commence his university degree, so hopefully they'll be looking for somebody to replace him! Please write and tell me what your plans are for the summer. Are you going to visit that Spanish girl you encountered at Easter?

Lots of love,

Megan

6 Make a list of activities, real or imaginary, that you plan to do this summer. Try to think of three for each of these topics.

    a travel
    b sports and hobbies
    c work and study
    d time with friends

7 Make a paragraph plan. Choose the most interesting of your ideas for each topic in 6. Then add notes to give more details of times, places, people, etc.

8 Imagine you received a letter from an English-speaking friend, ending like Chloe's in 1. Read the **how to do it** box, then write your own answer, using your plan from 7.

how to do it

Read the task carefully and underline the key words.
Brainstorm ideas and select the best ones.
Organise your ideas and make a paragraph plan.
Link sentences and paragraphs where appropriate.

Review

1 Complete sentences a–f with the most appropriate adjective from 1–6.

1 bossy   4 argumentative
2 loyal   5 sensitive
3 sensible   6 easy-going

a Be careful what you say to Harry – he's quite .... and gets upset very easily.

b You're always telling me what to do. I wish you weren't so .... !

c Hannah is a very .... friend – I know I can always rely on her to be there for me.

d Kelly is so .... that she never really gets angry or upset about anything.

e Judy is very .... – she'll ask somebody the time and then disagree with them.

f Think carefully before you make a decision. I know that you will, you're very ....

2 Correct any mistakes with the underlined verb forms in five of these sentences.

a Let's meet at the theatre tonight. The play <u>is starting</u> at 7.30.

b I'll probably be exhausted by the time I reach Edinburgh because <u>I'll have been driving</u> all morning.

c I can't go shopping with you tomorrow morning – <u>I'll have</u> my hair cut.

d By the time the next World Cup comes around, some of our most talented footballers <u>won't have played</u> any longer.

e <u>I'll be standing</u> here until you apologise for what you just said.

f <u>Will you have been leaving</u> by the time we get to the hotel?

3 Complete the sentences with the present or future simple of the verb in brackets.

a As soon as we .... (arrive), we'll let you know.

b It's impossible to be sure, but I don't think she .... (lose) her job.

c I .... (be) amazed if Real Madrid don't win tonight's match.

d The doctors are keeping me in hospital until they .... (know) what the problem is.

e The more money you spend now, the less you .... (have) for your holiday next week.

f Do you think your brother .... (help) us with our homework, if we ask him nicely?

4 Complete the text with the missing verbs.

Our relationships with our friends 1 .... an important part in our lives, and help us to 2 .... sense of the world. Megan has been a close friend of mine since primary school, and we're always together. In fact, some of our classmates 3 .... fun of us, saying that we're like identical twins. Occasionally, we 4 .... a row, but we never really fall out. The important thing is being able to 5 .... sorry, if you know you are in the wrong.

5 Rewrite each sentence a–d keeping the meaning the same. Use two to five words including the word given.

a Before we made a final decision, we considered everybody's opinion.
account
We .... before making a final decision.

b Will you promise me that you won't tell anybody?
word
Will you .... that you won't tell anybody?

c I contacted an old school friend after seeing his details on a website.
touch
Having seen an old school friend's details on a website, I .... him.

d Only people who have participated in a triathlon can fully understand the excitement.
part
The only way to understand fully the excitement of a triathlon is .... one.

Wild

Lead in

1 🔊 Listen to five people talking about where they live. For each one say if they

- live in a city.
- live in the countryside.
- are happy with where they live.

2 🔊 Choose the correct word to complete each sentence a–g from the listening in 1. Then listen again and check.

a The *sight/view* from my bedroom window is fantastic.
b I'm *right/very* in the middle of everything.
c The *scene/scenery* around here is amazing.
d I feel so *insulated/isolated* here.
e There are no *features/facilities* nearby.
f There's no sense of *community/society*.
g I love the peace and *quiet/quietness*.

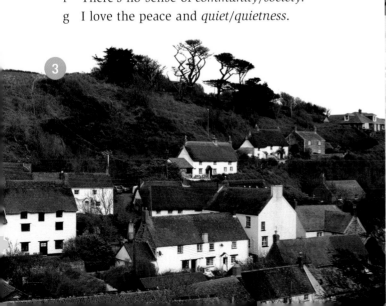

3 Describe the photos and say how life would be different in each place. Use these adjectives to help you.

busy   cosmopolitan   crowded   isolated
noisy   peaceful   rural   urban

4 In pairs, take it in turns to describe where you live and what you like or dislike about it. Include words and phrases from 2 and 3 if possible.

Reading

Part 3 Multiple matching

1 Look at the photos. Using a dictionary if necessary, say which of the four animals shown

   a walk on all fours.   d is a herbivore.
   b lives in a herd.   e has hands with palms.
   c eats roots and nuts.   f might help a shepherd.

2 You are going to read about four children who were raised by animals. Read the text quickly to find out

   a where each child was found.
   b how old each child was when they were found.

how to do it

Read the whole text once. If there are no section headings, it may help to add your own.

Read the questions. Answer any that you can immediately and underline the relevant parts of the text. You do not need to read these again.

Read each section of the text carefully, looking for answers to all the remaining questions.

3 Read the **how to do it** box. Then read the text again carefully, and for questions 1–15, choose from the children A–D. The children may be chosen more than once.

Which child

  1 could run and jump very fast?
  2 looked younger when captured than he really was?
  3 claims a group of wild animals gave him food?
  4 hardly ever stood upright?
  5 eventually returned to live in his family home?
  6 had unusual feet?
  7 was not familiar with some common kinds of food?
  8 has been seen by many different experts?
  9 did not go back to live with humans?
  10 was very violent towards the people who captured him?
  11 learned from animals how to look for things to eat?
  12 was taken by a wild animal when very young?
  13 only seemed to eat plants?
  14 reacted like a wild animal to sudden sounds?
  15 copied the social rules and body language of the animals he lived with?

4 Find phrasal verbs a–f in the text and use the context to match them with their meanings (1–6).

   a bring up (l. 1)   1 find
   b come across (l. 6)   2 remove
   c come up to (l. 12)   3 take care of
   d take away (l. 38)   4 raise (a child)
   e keep up (l. 46)   5 approach
   f look after (l. 62)   6 go at the same speed

5 Use the ideas below to discuss what feral children might find difficult about rejoining society.

  • eating and drinking
  • games and playing
  • family and friends
  • school and education

BORN TO BE WILD

For centuries, people have told stories about children who were brought up by animals and became like animals themselves: so-called 'feral children'. *Tarzan of the Apes* and *The Jungle Book* are two famous fictional accounts. There are many other accounts which claim to be true, although it is sometimes difficult to separate fact from fantasy and folklore.

One day in 1991, a Ugandan villager called Milly Sebba went further than usual in search of firewood, and came across a little boy with a group of monkeys. She summoned help and the boy was captured and brought back to Milly's village. A villager identified the boy as John Sesebunya, last seen in 1988 at the age of two or three. Later, John claimed that he had got lost in the forest, and that he remembered monkeys coming up to him after a few days and offering him roots and nuts. The pack of five monkeys taught him, he says, to search for food and to climb trees. John has been studied by a host of scientists, who are convinced that he is a genuine feral child. When left with a group of monkeys he avoids eye contact and approaches them from the side with open palms, just as monkeys do.

Jean-Claude Auger, an anthropologist from the Basque country, was travelling alone across the Spanish Sahara in 1960 when he met some Nemadi nomads. They told him about a young boy who lived with a herd of gazelles. After searching for several days, Auger managed to find the herd and the boy. The boy was about 10 years old and walked on all fours, only standing occasionally. Whenever there was an unexpected noise, he twitched his nose and ears, just like the rest of the herd. One senior female seemed to act as his adoptive mother. He would eat roots with his teeth and appeared to be herbivorous. When Auger chased the boy in a jeep to see how fast he could run, he reached a speed of 50 kilometres per hour, with leaps of about four metres. Unlike most of the feral children of whom there are records, the gazelle boy was never taken away from his wild companions.

A leopard-boy was reported by EC Stuart Baker in the Journal of the Bombay Natural History Society (July 1920). According to his report, the boy was stolen from his parents by a leopardess in the North Cachar Hills in India in about 1912, and three years later he was recovered and identified. At that time, the child, who was now five, could run on all fours so fast that an adult man could barely keep up. His knees had hard skin on them and his toes were bent upright, almost at right angles to his feet. The palms of his hands and pads of his toes and thumbs were also covered with very tough skin. When he was first caught, he bit and fought with everyone. If he came across a chicken in the village, he caught it, tore it into pieces and ate it with astonishing speed, just like a wild animal.

A feral child was caught in the Brasov region of Transylvania, Romania, in February 2002. Early one morning, shepherd Manolescu Ioan came upon a naked, wild-eyed child living in a cardboard box and covered with a plastic sheet. Manolescu reported his find to the police, who later captured the boy. It was believed he had lived alone in the forest for years, but doctors thought that he must have had some protection; perhaps he had been looked after by some of the many wild dogs in the region. He was the size of a normal four-year-old, but his missing front milk teeth suggested an actual age of seven. He ate whatever he was given, but didn't recognise fruit. About a week after his capture, he was identified as Traian Caldarar, lost three years earlier at the age of four. After being re-educated at an orphanage in Brasov, he was reunited with his mother, who lived in a remote village a few kilometres from where he had been found.

1

Vocabulary

Describing natural landscapes

1 Look at the photos. Say whether there are landscapes like these in your country and where, and in which other countries you might find them.

2 Identify one word which doesn't belong in each group a–e. Then explain the difference between the three words in the same group. Use a dictionary if necessary.

a	dune	mountain	hill	valley
b	lagoon	desert	lake	pond
c	field	forest	wood	jungle
d	beach	shore	coast	plain
e	bush	hedge	waterfall	tree

3 Match as many of the nouns in 2 as possible with the photos.

4 Imagine that you want to do the activities below with a friend from England. Say where in your country would be particularly good to do each one and why.

- mountain biking
- walking
- kayaking
- wind-surfing
- climbing

2

3

4

Grammar

Verb patterns GR p167

1 Read the first paragraph of the article opposite, which is about survival in the wilderness. Underline all the examples of infinitives (with and without *to*) and –*ing* forms, and circle the verbs which come immediately before them.

2 Put the verbs that you circled in 1 into Group A or B, depending on the verb pattern.
- Group A   verb + –*ing* form   *enjoy*
- Group B   verb + infinitive   *expect*

3 Complete gaps 1–12 in the article with the infinitive or –*ing* form of the verbs in brackets.

4 For each of 1–4, decide which sentence, a or b, makes most sense in the gap.

1 .... I'm sure he's very interesting.
   a   I wish my neighbour would stop talking.
   b   I wish my neighbour would stop to talk.

2 .... He therefore had no way of getting in touch with her.
   a   He didn't remember to write down the woman's phone number.
   b   He didn't remember writing down the woman's phone number.

3 .... However, the room still felt too hot.
   a   He tried to open the window.
   b   He tried opening the window.

4   William Faulkner began his career by writing short stories. ....
   a   He went on to write novels.
   b   He went on writing novels.

5 Complete these sentences in two different ways, once with an infinitive and once with an –*ing* form. Try to use a different verb each time.

a   When I leave school, I'll go on …
b   I wish people would stop …
c   I think I should try …
d   I'll always remember …

SURVIVING IN THE WILDERNESS

Many people enjoy travelling through wild and deserted landscapes, but few expect to end up in a genuine survival situation. The unexpected occasionally happens, however, so you should be prepared. Imagine finding yourself in the middle of a wilderness with a broken-down jeep and hardly any food and water. What should your priorities be? Should you stay with your vehicle and hope to be rescued? Or should you search for civilisation and risk getting even more lost? Should you spend time searching for water or food first? Or should you postpone worrying about food and water until you have managed to find or build a shelter? If you are not sure, keep reading – this article could save your life!

PRIORITY 1 SHELTER

Do not put off [1] .... (make) a shelter – it should be your first priority. Try [2] .... (enlarge) an existing, natural shelter, such as a hole in the ground below a fallen tree. If you happen [3] .... (be) near a rocky coast, build a shelter and cover it with wood from the beach. If you are on the move, stop [4] .... (build) your shelter while it is still light.

PRIORITY 2 WATER

If you fail [5] .... (find) water, you will only survive for about three days (whereas you can survive for weeks without food). If there is no rain, try [6] .... (walk) through vegetation early in the morning to collect moisture in clothing. Avoid [7] .... (drink) water that looks or smells bad.

PRIORITY 3 FIRE

Fire has many uses. It makes food more appetising. If you can't face [8] .... (eat) raw worms, boil them in water to make a nourishing soup! Fire protects against dangerous animals, since many will not dare [9] .... (approach) it. And you can also use it for signalling to rescuers – before they give up [10] .... (look) for you!

PRIORITY 4 FOOD

It is quite easy to get food in the wild, if you know where to look. Many survival books suggest [11] .... (eat) a small amount of unknown plants to test if they are poisonous. However, we do not recommend [12] .... (do) this, since some plants are so poisonous that even a very small amount can cause serious health problems.

Listening

Part 2 Sentence completion

1 Read the paragraph below and explain in your own words what 'Wilderness Therapy' is.

Wilderness Therapy

REDCLIFF ASCENT is located in a remote area of desert and red rock in the state of Utah. It offers 'wilderness therapy' to troubled teenagers, 'helping them and their families find a new beginning'. Life there is not easy – it certainly isn't a holiday. During their stay, the students live a nomadic lifestyle, walking five to 10 kilometres each day from camp to camp. They have to build their own shelters for sleeping in, cook their own food and wash their own clothes: in short, to take full responsibility for their survival. They also learn how to work together in a group to solve problems. In the evenings, they sit round the fire and talk about their experiences. Education is an important part of RedCliff Ascent, and it focuses on seven key values: courage, self-discipline, respect, honesty, work ethic, trust and compassion.

courage
self-discipline
respect
honesty
work ethic
trust
compassion

2 ◉)) Listen once to the stories of two teenagers Rachael and Ed, to find out who had the more positive experience at RedCliff Ascent.

3 ◉)) Listen again and complete sentences 1–10.
1 Many of the teenagers who go to RedCliff Ascent have broken the _____ .
2 The parents of many of the teenagers had no idea how to _____ their children.
3 At school, Rachael had been keen on long-distance _____ .
4 After returning from RedCliff, Rachael decided that she wanted to work with _____ .
5 Rachael continues to have a good relationship with her _____ .
6 Rachael's mother thinks that now Rachael looks really _____ .
7 Ed caused so many problems for his family that he had to find another _____ .
8 Ed's mother, Jane, says that Ed always wants more _____ .
9 Two weeks after the camp finished, Ed once again started _____ .
10 Ed's mother is hopeful that his second stay at RedCliff will be _____ .

4 Discuss why you think Wilderness Therapy is successful for many out-of-control teenagers.

Speaking

Part 2

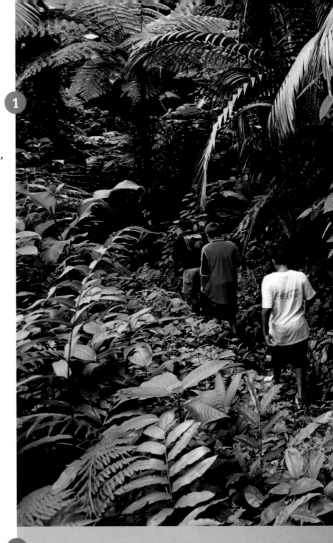

1 Look at the photos. Say whether sentences a–f describe photo 1, photo 2 or both.

a The people appear to be exploring a remote landscape.
b The weather is bright and sunny.
c There is a lot of dense vegetation.
d They're higher than some of the clouds.
e The ground is hard and rocky.
f There are snow-capped mountains in the distance.

2 Describe what the people are doing and wearing by making a sentence about photo 1 or photo 2 using a–g.

a jungle
b mountain range
c mountain bikes
d on foot
e in single file
f side by side
g long-sleeved jackets
h short-sleeved T-shirts
i spectacular scenery
j dense vegetation

3 •)) Listen to five people talking about the photos. Say which photo each speaker is talking about and note down the words that give you the answers.

4 •)) Listen again and complete these phrases.

a I think the people could be feeling quite ....
b Personally, I would be .... in their situation.
c I .... that they might be feeling quite tired.
d I love that .... of achievement you get from climbing up really high.
e It looks as .... they're quite bored.
f I hate the .... of not being able to see very far ahead.
g They .... be feeling really excited.
h They're .... feeling a bit hot and sweaty.

5 Compare the photos and say

a which holiday activity is more challenging, and why.
b why you think the people chose each particular type of holiday.
c which holiday you would enjoy more, and why.

Use of English

1 Phrases a and b can complete sentences 1–6 below, with similar meanings. Choose the correct preposition for each phrase, using a dictionary if necessary.

1 Many teenagers are _____ Internet chat rooms.

   a addicted *on/to*   b hooked *on/to*

2 People who smoke are _____ developing serious health problems.

   a *at/in* danger of   b *at/in* risk of

3 The streets in the town centre are _____ litter.

   a full *of/with*   b covered *of/with*

4 Nobody knew _____ his strange behaviour at the restaurant.

   a the reason *of/for*   b the cause *of/for*

5 The head teacher wanted to introduce school uniforms, but most of the teachers were not _____ .

   a *in/of* agreement   b *in/of* the same opinion

6 To be truly a great artist you cannot be _____ failure.

   a frightened *with/of*   b worried *about/of*

> **tip** Prepositions are often difficult to use correctly because there are few rules. Try to learn them as part of longer phrases.

2 Choose the correct prepositions to complete a–i.

a My girlfriend arrived *at/to* the cinema ten minutes late.

b Whether progress is always a good thing depends *of/on* your point of view.

c People usually dress *in/with* colourful clothes at carnivals.

d The protests have had no effect *on/to* the government.

e Madonna is married *to/with* a film director.

f This shirt was made *with/by* hand.

g The film *300* is based *in/on* a true story.

h Australians are very good *at/in* many sports.

i Some websites are popular all *across/over* the world.

3 Read the text quickly, ignoring the gaps, to find out why some people think Cute Knut should not have been allowed to live.

Cute Knut

Everyone loves Knut. The three-month-old polar bear, born in (0) *one* of Berlin's zoos, has become a star in the German capital and has won fans (1) _____ over the world. It's impossible not to adore the little guy, right? Well, not quite. Animal rights activists aren't so in love (2) _____ the polar bear baby. They are concerned that Knut, who is being raised by human hand after his mother rejected him, is (3) _____ danger of losing touch with his natural identity. Some people (4) _____ like to see him dead.

'Raising a wild animal (5) _____ hand is against animal welfare laws,' animal rights activist Frank Albrecht told the press. 'The zoo needs to kill the bear cub,' he added. Unsurprisingly, this view has not been popular (6) _____ the general public. But Wolfram Graf-Rudolf, director of the Aachen Zoo, is (7) _____ the same opinion, although he feels it is now (8) _____ late to put Knut out of his supposed misery. 'The mistake has been made. They should (9) _____ had the courage to kill him much earlier.'

The zoo reports that little Knut is becoming a bit of a handful as (10) _____ gets bigger – suggesting that the bear is maybe not as human (11) _____ some people fear. 'His keeper is covered (12) _____ bruises, which shows that Knut has discovered he is a bear,' said the zoo's management.

4 Read the **how to do it** box. Then read the text again carefully and complete gaps 1–12 with one word each.

how to do it

Read the title and the text quickly for the general meaning. Don't fill in any gaps yet.

Read the text again, slowly, and try to fill in the missing words. Look at the words around the gap and try to work out what part of speech the missing word is.

Read the completed text to check your spelling and overall sense.

5 Discuss whether zoos are a good or bad thing, giving examples.

Vocabulary

Collective nouns

1 Put these nouns into groups a–d according to their collective nouns.

bananas	birds	cards	dogs	cows
elephants	flowers	sheep		

a   a flock of ....

b   a herd of ....

c   a pack of ....

d   a bunch of ....

2 Match nouns a–h with the groups of people they describe (1–8).

a   audience   1   people acting in a play or film

b   cast   2   people who play sport together, or work together

c   crew   3   people working in an organisation

d   crowd   4   people watching a film, concert, play, etc.

e   gang   5   a group of experts

f   panel   6   a large group of people

g   staff   7   people working on a ship or a plane

h   team   8   a group of people who may cause trouble

3 Complete these sentences with collective nouns from 1 and 2.

a   Apparently a fight broke out last night between two .... of football fans.

b   As we ate our lunch in the park, a .... of pigeons circled round and landed next to us.

c   We had to stop the car when we came across a farmer driving a .... of cows down the lane.

d   Hospital .... have threatened to go on strike unless they receive a pay rise.

e   The .... of the show includes some big Hollywood stars.

f   I always send my girlfriend a .... of roses on Valentine's Day.

g   A .... gathered outside the cinema, hoping to see the stars at the film premiere.

h   The .... sat spellbound throughout the entire concert.

Writing

Part 1 A formal email

1 Read the email below to find out what two questions Jennifer has about the archaeological expedition.

> **New Message**
>
> Send   Chat   Attach   Address   Fonts   Colors   Save As Draft
>
> **To:** INFO@HUARODIG
>
> **From:** JENNIFER MASON
>
> **Subject:** ARCHAEOLOGICAL EXPEDITION TO HUARO VALLEY
>
> I recently saw your advertisement requesting volunteers for the forthcoming archaeological dig in Peru, and I should very much like to take part in the expedition.
>
> Although I hold no formal qualifications in archaeology, I have been on a number of archaeological digs and have acquired a good knowledge of the processes involved. I consider myself to be a good team player and am also enthusiastic and adventurous.
>
> I have two queries about the expedition. Firstly, it wasn't clear exactly how long volunteers were expected to stay in Peru. Secondly, could you give me a clearer impression of the level of physical challenge the holiday would involve? Although I am physically fit, I would not consider myself particularly athletic. Would I be able to cope with this expedition?
>
> I would be grateful if you could address these queries before the weekend, as I am keen to finalise my holiday plans soon.
>
> Thank you.
>
> Jennifer Mason

2 Find these words in the email, which are all quite formal, and explain their meaning.

  a requesting
  b forthcoming
  c hold
  d acquired
  e impression
  f challenge
  g address

> **tip** Emails can be formal or informal, depending on who is writing to who. Use language appropriate to the context and do not mix registers.

3 Match the beginnings (a–e) and endings (1–5) of these requests for information, and explain the meaning of the underlined words.

  a I am writing to <u>request</u>
  b I would be <u>most</u> grateful if
  c A <u>prompt</u> reply to this email
  d I look forward to
  e <u>Further to</u> our recent telephone conversation,

  1 <u>hearing</u> from you.
  2 you could <u>respond to</u> these <u>queries</u> <u>swiftly</u>.
  3 could you <u>clarify</u> how much money you <u>require</u> as a deposit?
  4 <u>further</u> information about the trip featured on your website.
  5 would be appreciated.

4 Imagine you have seen this advertisement on a website. Read it along with your notes.
Then write an email of 120–150 words volunteering to take part and requesting information.

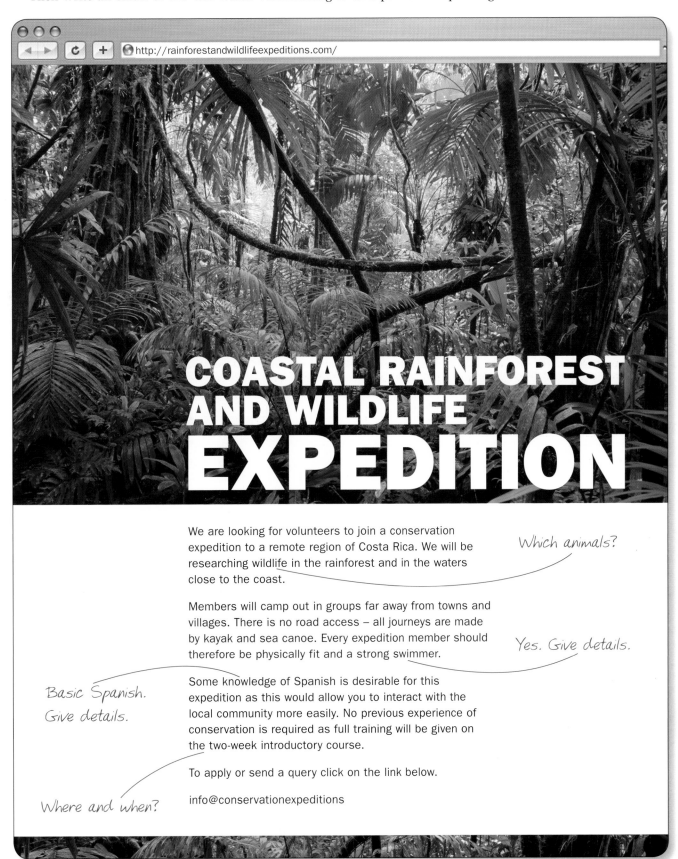

http://rainforestandwildlifeexpeditions.com/

COASTAL RAINFOREST AND WILDLIFE EXPEDITION

We are looking for volunteers to join a conservation expedition to a remote region of Costa Rica. We will be researching wildlife in the rainforest and in the waters close to the coast.

Which animals?

Members will camp out in groups far away from towns and villages. There is no road access – all journeys are made by kayak and sea canoe. Every expedition member should therefore be physically fit and a strong swimmer.

Yes. Give details.

Basic Spanish. Give details.

Some knowledge of Spanish is desirable for this expedition as this would allow you to interact with the local community more easily. No previous experience of conservation is required as full training will be given on the two-week introductory course.

To apply or send a query click on the link below.

info@conservationexpeditions

Where and when?

Review

1 **For a–e form words from the letters in brackets to complete the sentences.**

a The _____ (lawratfel) plunged 100 metres into the _____ (lavyel) below.

b To reach the lost city, the explorers had to swim across a wide _____ (noolag) and cut through thick _____ (lenjug).

c Although the _____ (toasc) is very beautiful, there are few _____ (scebaeh) where you can swim safely.

d Golden _____ (nesud) streched for miles across the _____ (steder).

e There's a small _____ (nodp) in our garden, surrounded by _____ (seshub).

2 **Complete sentences a–h with the infinitive or *–ing* form of these words, as appropriate.**

arrive eat go relax smoke see study walk

a My grandfather found it very difficult to give up _____ after forty years.

b Most people enjoy _____ at home at the weekend.

c After he finishes school, my brother hopes _____ History at university.

d She put off _____ the dentist, even though she had toothache.

e I'd suggest _____ to Portugal in the spring, before it gets too hot.

f I can't face _____ any breakfast before 8 o'clock in the morning.

g He called the police, but they failed _____ before the burglar had escaped.

h You should avoid _____ through Central Park alone at night.

3 **Choose the correct form of the verb to complete each of these sentences.**

a He left school at the age of 18 and went on *to do/ doing* a degree at Cambridge.

b They started playing tennis after lunch and went on *to play/playing* until it was nearly dark.

c Nobody answered the door when he knocked, so he tried *to tap/tapping* on the window.

d She tried *to move/moving* the bed but couldn't, because it was too heavy.

e He walked halfway down the street and then stopped *to tie/tying* his shoes.

f Would you please stop *to talk/talking* and listen!

4 **Complete gaps 1–5 in the text with the correct prepositions.**

It's easy to become hooked **1**_____ the feeling you get when you're up a mountain. While your everyday life might be full **2**_____ problems – you may be worried **3**_____ your bank balance, or **4**_____ risk of losing your job – the experience of standing on a mountain-top has a strange effect **5**_____ most people. They immediately forget their troubles and begin to feel on top of the world!

What's so funny?

Lead in

1 In pairs, discuss whether each of a–f is likely to make you laugh out loud, smile, or not even smile. Give reasons.

   a a Mr Bean film

   b a comedy cartoon, such as *The Simpsons*

   c a TV show of viewers' camcorder clips

   d a sitcom, such as *Friends*

   e a funny story told by a classmate

   f a joke told by a parent, uncle or aunt

2 In pairs, talk about the following. Give reasons, then see if you can agree on one for each idea.

   a a TV comedy that you like

   b a comedy actor that you find funny

   c a favourite joke

   d a classmate with a good sense of humour

   e a TV or film comedy that you don't find at all funny

3 Discuss what other kinds of things make you laugh out loud or smile.

4 Discuss whether a–e affect what people find funny. Where possible give examples.

   a how old they are

   b whether they're male or female

   c where they come from

   d what their family members find humorous

   e whether they are extrovert or introvert

Reading

Part 2 Gapped text

1 What's your favourite joke? Tell each other in groups and see if you can agree on the funniest.

2 Read the text below quickly, ignoring the gaps, to find out how the picture relates to it.

Here's one that you haven't heard...

THE SEARCH involved travel abroad, a website, 40,000 printable jokes, more than two million ratings from 70 countries, a year's exhaustive breakdown of humour by age, sex and nationality, 5 and a brain scan of someone listening to jokes.

Laughlab, an experiment set up more than a year ago, established that the British, Irish, New Zealanders and Australians prefer a play on words and that the French, Danes and Belgians have 10 a taste for the surreal. (1)...... The Germans apparently have the broadest sense of humour – if only because they have no national preference, and therefore find almost anything funny.

'It has been a fascinating year,' said Richard 15 Wiseman, a psychologist at the University of Hertfordshire, and founder of Laughlab. 'But if I hear one more joke I'm going to punch someone. It has been like being trapped in the back of a taxi with a driver who constantly says, 'Here's one that you have 20 never heard. (2)......'

The study reached a climax yesterday when a PhD student, dressed as a giant chicken, unveiled the world's funniest joke before the cameras in Covent Garden, London. The winning joke was the product of 25 international selection including ratings by website visitors. (3)...... This joke, according to Dr Wiseman, appealed to all. It also contained the three elements that were found central to humour: a sense of superiority, an unexpected response, and a sad 30 feeling of mortality. The joke was this:

> *A couple of New Jersey hunters are out in the woods when one of them falls to the ground. He doesn't seem to be breathing, his eyes are rolled back in his head. The other guy whips out his mobile phone and calls*
> 35 *the emergency services. He gasps to the operator: 'My friend is dead! What can I do?' The operator, in a calm, soothing voice says: 'Just take it easy. I can help. First, let's make sure he's dead.' There is a silence, then a shot is heard. The guy's voice comes back on the*
> 40 *line. He says: 'OK, now what?'*

DR GOSALL had liked the joke for years. He said: 'It makes people feel better ... reminds you that there's always someone out there doing something more stupid than you.' It was one of a
45 series of jokes read to a volunteer who was being given a brain scan. With each joke, a specific area at the front of the volunteer's brain lit up. (4)...... 'It fits in with other research, because if people have damage to that part of the brain, then they lose their
50 sense of humour,' Dr Wiseman said.

There were other discoveries. In a study of British regional variation, the Welsh were the keenest on jokes in general, and the Scots were the least keen. One joke – 'What's brown and sticky? A stick' – was
55 submitted 300 times, and nobody ever found it funny. Dr Wiseman also read out Laughlab's candidate for worst joke:

'Knock knock.'
'Who's there?'
65 'Boo.'
60 'Boo who?'
'Don't cry.'

The LaughLab computers counted the number of words in every joke that people submitted. (5)...... Interestingly, the winning 'hunters' joke is 102 words long – almost the perfect length for a joke!

70 Many of the jokes submitted contained references to animals. The researchers found that jokes mentioning ducks were seen as funnier than other jokes. (6)...... Regardless, the implication is clear – if you are going to tell a joke involving an animal, make it a duck.

75 (7)...... Careful analysis of the data revealed that people found the jokes funniest on the 7th October at 6.03 in the evening. Perhaps they have scientifically discovered the funniest moment of the year!

3 Read the text again carefully and the **tip** box. Then complete gaps 1–7 with sentences A–H, using the underlined words to help you. There is one extra sentence.

A According to the data, jokes containing 103 are the funniest.

B There was also a reaction in an area linked to memory, showing recognition of an old joke.

C The Laughlab computers also recorded the date and time that each person from the UK rated the jokes in LaughLab.

D But only the best jokes from each country were included in the survey.

E Quite frankly, I've had enough.

F It was posted by Gurpal Gosall, a 31-year-old psychiatrist from Manchester.

G Perhaps it's because of their beaks, or webbed feet, or odd shape.

H Americans and Canadians, on the other hand, chuckle at jokes showing one group's superiority over another.

4 Explain how the underlined words in A–H helped you to match the sentences with the gaps. Which other words helped you do the task?

5 Find the nationality words in the text to complete 1–8.

Country	Nationality	People
Australia	Australian	1
Belgium	Belgian	2
Denmark	Danish	3
France	French	4
Ireland	Irish	5
New Zealand	New Zealand	6
Scotland	Scottish	7
Wales	Welsh	8

6 Discuss whether any topic can be funny, or if there are some which should never be the subject of jokes.

Vocabulary

Extreme adjectives

1 Match adjectives a–l with their extreme forms below.

ancient	astounded	boiling	exhausted
filthy	freezing	furious	gorgeous
hideous	hilarious	spotless	starving

a attractive   g surprised
b ugly   h funny
c dirty   i angry
d clean   j tired
e hot   k old
f cold   l hungry

2 Work in pairs to find as many extreme adjectives as possible for a–d.

a very big
b very small
c very good
d very bad

3 Decide which of the words in a–e correctly completes each sentence.

a The cooker was *a bit/very/totally* spotless when Steve had finished cleaning it.

b Kate missed her appointment because her train was *extremely/totally/utterly* late.

c Put your hat and scarf on. It's *absolutely/extremely/very* freezing out there.

d Josh was feeling *quite/totally/absolutely* tired by the time he got home from work.

e I'm *completely/utterly/very* sorry, but I've forgotten your name.

Grammar

Past tenses GR p166–167

1 Choose the correct tense to complete a–h. Explain your choice, using the Grammar Reference section if necessary.

a *I've done/I've been doing* the ironing. I've only got three more shirts to do.

b When I phoned Karen, she was worried because her brother *didn't arrive/hadn't arrived* home.

c I've never tried Vietnamese food, but I *had/I've had* Thai.

d I *found/was finding* a wallet when I was walking home from the shops.

e Harry was sweating by the time he arrived at the cinema because he *had been/was running*.

f Have you ever *ridden/been riding* a horse?

g By the time we found the restaurant, it *closed/had closed*.

h At the time of the accident, George *wasn't wearing/didn't wear* a seatbelt.

2 Correct the mistakes in sentences a–h.

a I've never been believing in Santa Claus.

b I've been asking him three times, but he hasn't told me yet.

c Rita and Ahmed have arrived two minutes ago.

d By the time the fire brigade arrived, the fire had burnt for over an hour.

e How long have you studied Chinese?

f According to the police, the thieves have left the country a few hours after committing the crime.

g How often have you been travelling by plane?

h My aunt isn't here yet, but my uncle has arrived last night.

3 Complete sentences a–h with your own ideas, using an appropriate tense.

a   I've never tried bungee jumping, but ....

b   Julie's hair was wet because ....

c   As they were getting onto the train, ...

d   By the time we arrived at the shop, ...

e   I .... since 8 o'clock this morning.

f   She .... three times this year.

g   He opened the door, ran outside and ....

h   At midnight last night, George ....

4 Complete the text with an appropriate form of the verbs in brackets. Sometimes more than one tense is possible.

By the time I *arrived* (arrived) at the wedding, many of the guests
¹ .... (go) home. Monica ² .... (sit) on the stairs, red-eyed. She
³ .... (cry), but she was OK now. 'I ⁴ .... (wait) for a taxi since
ten o'clock,' she explained. 'I ⁵ .... (phone) three times, but it ⁶ ....
(not come).' I ⁷ .... (offer) her a lift home and she ⁸ .... (accept).
As we ⁹ .... (walk) to my car, she ¹⁰ .... (touch) my hand gently.
'I ¹¹ .... (think) about you a lot recently,' she said. 'You're one of
the kindest people I ¹² .... (meet) in my life.'

5 Continue the story in 4 with your own ideas. Start with the words 'At that moment, …' and end with 'we both laughed'. Write 60–80 words.

Listening

Part 1 Multiple choice

1 In pairs, discuss which of these situations might make you laugh. If possible, give an example.

a you feel nervous
b you make a mistake
c you see somebody else make a mistake
d you feel embarrassed
e you're trying to be polite
f you get a sudden fright

2 Read the first line only of questions 1–8 in 3 below and match each situation with extracts a–h.

a 'Did you go to Justin's on New Year's Eve?'
b 'The arrested man has been named as Robert Winchester.'
c '"Unmissable" according to *Time* magazine.'
d 'As we were walking past the graveyard, we noticed a figure standing by a gravestone.'
e 'Have you heard the one about the tortoise?'
f 'What are you going to sing for us today?'
g 'I have a copy of your CV here.'
h 'They asked 97 volunteers to watch various film extracts, and secretly taped their laughter.'

3 �))) You will hear people talking in eight different situations. For questions 1–8, choose the correct answer (A, B, or C).

1 You hear a man telling a joke.
What is the joke about?
A A detective and a snail.
B A group of detectives in New York.
C A tortoise and some snails.

2 You hear a newsreader making a mistake in a news item.
What is the item about?
A A crime at the Prime Minister's home.
B Improved security at the Prime Minister's home.
C An injury to a detective during an arrest.

3 You hear a woman being interviewed for a job. Why did the woman leave her first job?
A Because she fell asleep while working and was fired.
B Because she went to work for another furniture company.
C Because the company had to close all its shops.

4 You hear a report about a scientific study. What surprised the researchers?
A They had thousands of bursts of laughter to analyse.
B There were a lot of different sounds in the laughter.
C The women laughed more often than the men.

5 You hear a boy and a girl talking at a party. Where have they seen each other before?
A at school
B at Martin's house
C at another party

6 You hear a man telling a scary story.
What does the old woman in the story say?
A She says, 'What do you want?'
B She says, 'Suddenly, my heart started thumping.'
C We don't know what she says.

7 You hear a radio advertisement for a film.
What kind of film is it?
A a love story
B a comedy
C a documentary about holidays

8 You hear a man called Brian give an audition in a talent show.
What does the judge think of Brian?
A He's confident, but that's all.
B He's got the right look, but he can't sing.
C He hasn't got a good voice or any confidence.

Speaking

Parts 3 and 4

1 Look at the photos. Have you seen any of these forms of entertainment in the past year? Tell a partner about them.

2 ◀)) Listen to two people arranging a night out and say which of the phrases for making suggestions (a–i) you hear. What do they decide to book tickets for?

a Let's go to …
b Well, why don't we just go to … ?
c How does this sound? We go to …
d Shall we go and see … ?
e How about … ?
f I know. What about … ?
g I've got an idea. We could …
h Do you fancy going to see … ?
i Would you like to … ?

3 ◀)) Choose the correct words to complete these opinions. Then listen again and check.

a I don't *think/find* clowns very amusing.
b I'm not really *on/into* musicals.
c In *fact/effect*, I really don't like stage comedies at all.
d To be *honest/true*, silent films don't make me laugh.
e Romantic comedies aren't really my *thing/business*.
f I'm not a *strong/big* fan of comedy clubs.

4 Imagine that you are going out for the evening. Read the **how to do it** box, then in pairs, give your opinions of each form of entertainment shown and decide which one you are going to book tickets for. Use phrases from 2 and 3.

how to do it

Give your own opinions clearly and simply.
Listen to your partner and react to what they say.
Try to correct any mistakes you make, but don't spend time worrying about them.
Keep talking until the examiner stops you.

5 Answer these Part 4 questions with your own ideas and opinions.

a Is it more enjoyable seeing these types of entertainment on your own or with friends? Give reasons.
b What other forms of entertainment are popular with young people in your country?

Use of English

Part 1 Multiple-choice cloze

1 Discuss which of the adjectives below you would use to describe yourself and any brothers and sisters you have.

> adventurous   creative   humorous
> rebellious   risk-taking   unconventional

2 Read the newspaper report opposite ignoring the gaps, and choose the best heading (a, b or c).

a Famous comedians were funny children.
b Younger siblings have fewer skills.
c Younger siblings are more humorous.

3 Read the the **tip** box. Then read the text again carefully and decide which answer (A, B, C or D) best fits each gap.

> **C**hildren with older brothers and sisters find it easier to (0) *make* people laugh, a survey has suggested. Just over half of younger siblings who (1) ...... part in the survey said it was easy to be humorous, compared with a third of those who were (2) .... And just 11% of (3) ...... children had the skill, according to the study of 1,000 people by psychologist Richard Wiseman. 'Younger siblings have to compete (4) .... parental attention, so they have to be more unconventional. They are risk-taking, and also more humorous. On the other (5)...... , older children tend to take on much more serious roles. And of course children without siblings don't feel the (6) ...... to compete at all.'
>
> And (7) .... funny continues into adulthood. Younger siblings who (8) ...... to become famous comedians in Britain include Rowan Atkinson, better known as 'Mr Bean'.
>
> Professor Wiseman, who compiled the report, said his (9) ...... tie in with other research about the (10) ...... of family position on personality. He said University of California research had suggested that, because younger children had not had the chance to (11) ...... the same skills and abilities as their older siblings, they had to find novel ways of gaining attention. This (12) ...... to make them more creative, unconventional, adventurous and rebellious.

tip Try to think of possible answers before looking at the options.

0	A force	B push	C make	D encourage
1	A had	B took	C did	D played
2	A first-born	B major	C primary	D new born
3	A only	B unique	C single	D sole
4	A over	B on	C in	D for
5	A hand	B side	C way	D matter
6	A want	B idea	C need	D lack
7	A to be	B be	C being	D been
8	A put on	B went on	C took on	D came on
9	A happenings	B readings	C sayings	D findings
10	A cause	B effect	C reason	D logic
11	A develop	B increase	C enlarge	D grow
12	A intends	B extends	C tends	D sends

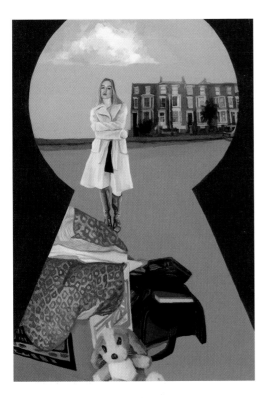

Vocabulary

Phrasal verbs with *put*

1 Complete sentences a–h with *up* or *down*.

  a I must find a new apartment. I can't put *up with/down with* my noisy neighbours any longer!

  b It's not surprising she lacks confidence. Her older siblings are always putting her *up/down*.

  c I couldn't find a hotel room, so my friend agreed to put me *up/down* for the night.

  d He was finding it difficult to sleep at night. At first, he put this *up to/down to* stress.

  e Armed rebels tried to overthrow the government, but the army soon put *up/down* the revolt.

  f I need several thousand euros to pay for a year abroad before university. Fortunately, my parents have agreed to put *up/down* half the amount.

  g Because of a shortage of oil and gas, energy companies have put *up/down* their prices.

  h He admitted vandalising the bus stop, but claimed his friends had put him *up to/down to* it.

2 Rewrite the sentences in 1 using the verbs below in an appropriate form instead of phrasal verbs. Use a dictionary to help you, if necessary.

accommodate   suppress   explain   humiliate
increase   persuade   provide   tolerate

3 In pairs, think of as many other phrasal verbs with *put* as you can. Then check in your dictionary.

4 Complete sentences a–h with phrasal verbs with *put*.

  a To be a good musician, you need to put .... hours of practice.

  b He's terrible at explaining things. He finds it impossible to put .... his points clearly.

  c These forest fires have been burning for days, despite all the efforts to put them ....

  d Is he really upset – or is he just putting it ....?

  e I still love her, despite everything that she's put me ....

  f The government has put .... a new plan to improve the transport system.

  g She's really messy. She never puts anything .... in its proper place.

  h I'd like to travel more, but all those delays at airports really put me ....

5 In pairs, talk about a–c.

  a things you've learned to do by putting in a lot of time

  b things that would put you off being friends with someone

  c things you don't enjoy but have to put up with

Writing

Part 2 A story

1 Read the story about a pilot. Find out why the passengers panic when they see him.

2 Read the story again and do the following.

   a Find an example of reported speech and rewrite it using direct speech.

   b Find an example of direct speech and rewrite it as reported speech.

3 Explain the difference between these pairs of reporting verbs and find three of them in the story.

   a explain   admit

   b remark   state

   c warn   advise

   d reply   add

   e promise   claim

A FUNNY STORY

A funny thing happened on a flight from Seattle to San Francisco. Unexpectedly, the plane stopped in Sacramento along the way. The flight attendant explained that there would be a delay, and if the passengers wanted to get off the aircraft, they could.

All the passengers got off the plane except for one gentleman, who was blind. He stayed in his seat, with his guide dog by his feet. A few minutes later, as the pilot was leaving the plane, he stopped in the aisle next to the blind man and remarked, 'We'll be in Sacramento for almost an hour. Would you like to get off and stretch your legs?' The blind man replied, 'No thanks, but my dog might like a walk. Would you mind taking him with you?'

All the people in the terminal building were horrified when they looked up and saw the pilot walking off the plane with a guide dog! The pilot was even wearing sunglasses. People panicked. Some of them were desperate to change airlines!

4 Rewrite the direct speech in a–e as indirect speech, using appropriate reporting verbs from 3.

Example   Jake: 'I cheated in the exam.'
          Jake admitted that he'd cheated in the exam.

a   Sarah: 'I've seen a UFO.'
b   Tom: 'I'll always be a loyal friend.'
c   Beth: 'The alarm will go off if you open that door!'
d   Denis: 'And what's more it's much too late to go out.'
e   Claire: 'My clothes are dirty because I've been cleaning my bike.'

5 Read this passage from another story, ignoring the underlined words. Complete each gap with the correct tense.

A very funny thing [1]............ (*was happening/happened/has happened*) to me last Saturday. It was about 5 p.m. and I [2]............ (*was sitting/sat/had sat*) at home watching a very good film on TV. I was feeling very tired as I [3]............ (*was playing/played/had been playing*) football all afternoon. The film [4]............ (*just finished/has just finished/was just finishing*) when there was a knock at the door. It was the driver of a very big lorry, which he [5]............ (*parked/ has parked/had parked*) in front of the house. He said that he [6]............ (*was having/had/had had*) a parcel for me.

tip   When you write a story, try to include some direct speech.
      Use a variety of speech-related verbs, not just *said*.
Try to use one or two extreme adjectives to make the story more vivid.

6 Read the paragraph in 5 again and do the following.
   a   Find an example of indirect speech and rewrite it as direct speech.
   b   Replace the underlined words with extreme adjectives.

7 Read the task below and the tip box, then write your story in 120–180 words.

Your teacher has asked you to write a story for an international magazine. The story must begin with these words. Choose a, b or c.

A funny thing happened…
a   during a lesson at school.
b   when I was out with my friends.
c   while I was shopping in town.

Review

1 Rewrite the text using extreme adjectives to replace the underlined phrases.

> Juliet sat on the edge of her bed. She looked at her bedroom floor. It was <u>very dirty</u>. She wanted to clean her room. She normally kept it <u>very clean</u>. But she felt <u>very tired</u>. Then she got a text message. She was <u>very surprised</u> when she read it. It was from Liam, the <u>very attractive</u> boy in her class. The message said: 'Fancy lunch? I'm <u>very hungry</u>.' Suddenly, Juliet felt more optimistic. 'Perhaps this isn't going to be a <u>very bad</u> day after all,' she thought, and gave a <u>very small</u> smile.

2 Choose the best word, a or b, to complete 1–5.

1 My aunt keeps her house .... spotless.
   a extremely   b totally

2 You should bring a jumper. It's .... freezing outside.
   a absolutely   b completely

3 We were .... sorry to hear about your accident.
   a very   b utterly

4 The train was .... late and we missed the start of the play.
   a utterly   b extremely

5 Harry was .... tired by the end of the race.
   a totally   b quite

3 Correct the phrasal verbs in a–h.

a The heat doesn't put me on going to Africa.

b Don't criticise me! You're always putting me through.

c I can't afford to shop there any more. They've put forward their prices.

d Put in your mobile until the lesson has finished!

e When he speaks French, he finds it hard to put out what he's trying to say.

f I wasn't really miserable. I was just putting it out.

g You'll pass the exam if you put away enough hours of revision.

h If you ever visit London, don't book a hotel room – we'll put you away for the night.

4 Read the text below and decide which answer (A, B, C or D) best fits each gap 1–12.

Although few students would say that school lessons and laughter ^{0} .... together, two Ohio University psychology professors argue that the use of humour in online courses can ^{1} .... good results. Mark Shatz and Frank LoSchiavo found that humour can significantly ^{2} .... student interest. 'We know students taking online courses often ^{3} .... them as boring and impersonal, ^{4} .... we thought about the idea of trying to incorporate humour into online teaching,' said Shatz. The study took an existing course and added humour in the ^{5} .... of jokes and cartoons. Forty-four students then did ^{6} .... the original course or the more humorous course, and the researchers studied their performance. They counted the number of times students ^{7} .... part in the online discussion. They also asked students to rate their overall enjoyment of the course. The ^{8} .... showed that students who did the more humourous course were more likely to make comments on discussion boards. They also seemed to enjoy the course more. 'Teachers don't need to be comedians,' said Shatz. 'Our job is not to ^{9} .... students laugh. Our job is to ^{10} .... them learn, and if humour can make learning more enjoyable, then everybody benefits.' On the other ^{11} ...., humour alone cannot save a poorly planned class, and too ^{12} .... humour can work against student learning. 'If I make my students laugh too hard, they're going to remember my funny story and not the material,' admitted Shatz.

0	A make	B (go)	C have	D do
1	A do	B make	C produce	D present
2	A grow	B rise	C increase	D multiply
3	A believe	B view	C think	D look
4	A that	B so	C as	D then
5	A way	B type	C form	D kind
6	A either	B both	C or	D neither
7	A took	B had	C played	D did
8	A happenings	B readings	C sayings	D findings
9	A force	B cause	C make	D create
10	A produce	B help	C teach	D get
11	A side	B way	C hand	D matter
12	A much	B many	C big	D good

Inspired

Lead in

1 Look at the photos and answer these questions about each person.
  a What different talents do they need?
  b Where might they get their inspiration from?
  c What kind of hard work do they each have to put in?
  d Who do you think has to work hardest to be successful?
  e Who do you admire most?

singer-songwriter

dancer

2 Using the ideas below, discuss which of the people shown you'd most like to be and why.

become famous
make money
work alone
create something beautiful
change the world
travel the world

3 In pairs, think of as many other professions as you can that require inspiration.

inventor/scientist

film director

WHEN THE MUSIC TAKES YOU

What do artists go through when they create, and does the process change them? *New Scientist* magazine asked leading songwriters Alex Kapranos of Franz Ferdinand and David Gray what inspiration feels like.

NS Can you describe the process you go through when you write songs?

Alex There are two very different stages. There is an initial creative stage where it all comes out. It feels a bit like the first time you ride a bicycle or drive a car. **1 ☐** You end up with this big sprawling mess of an idea. And then you have that other process which is a lot more controlled, where you get rid of all the parts that are irrelevant. During the first process you're not really considering what you're doing, you're just doing it. The actual writing of a song is fairly easy. But the second process is very ruthless and quite cold because you have to cut away things that you're attached to.

NS Do you write better in certain environments?

Alex I tend to write in all sorts of places. For our new record I've written songs in hotel rooms, on the back of tour buses, in corridors, wherever I've had an opportunity to sit down and pick up a guitar. **2 ☐** I usually just feel like doing it, and do it. It's usually either when you feel there's no pressure to be doing other things, or when you feel almost selfishly unaware of other things.

NS Are you a different person when you're writing?

Alex I find myself being rude to people when I'm trying to get past the distractions. I used to have big arguments with my mother. It's funny because I'm generally not rude at all, I'm generally very polite, probably too polite.

NS What does it feel like when you're writing?

Alex If it's good, it feels really exciting. It's like listening to a story you've never heard before. **3 ☐** All the everyday stuff – conversation, where you left your keys – it all seems to belong to a different brain, almost like a brain in somebody else's head. That's why the distractions are so infuriating, because it's like being reminded that this other brain exists.

Reading

Part 2 Gapped text

1 Look at the photos and answer these questions.

 a Can you name the people shown?

 b Do you know the name of any of their songs or albums?

2 Quickly read the first paragraph of the text opposite to check your answer to 1a.

3 Read the whole text carefully, then match sentences A–H with gaps 1–7. There is one extra sentence.

A As you follow it, you lose your sense of where you are.

B I'm not a particularly easy person to live with during these times.

C You're trying to control something but you're not quite sure which direction it's going.

D I never write songs when I'm in a bad mood.

E But sometimes you can tell, because all your emotions are stirred.

F Environment isn't particularly important.

G But occasionally a song just seems to come out of nowhere.

H At the same time, you open a door in your brain that is normally closed.

4 Find phrasal verbs a–g in the text and match them with meanings 1–7.

a end up (l. 11)
b turn into (l. 45)
c hang around (l. 46)
d pick up (l. 47)
e shut down (l. 49)
f think up (l. 61)
g start off (l. 68)

1 wait, not doing very much
2 begin
3 find yourself in an unexpected place or situation
4 stop something working
5 invent or create in your mind
6 take hold of
7 make something become something else

5 Read the dictionary entry for *think up*. How does the entry indicate that it is a separable phrasal verb?

> ˌthink sth↔'up (*informal*) to create sth in your mind
> **SYN** DEVISE, INVENT: *Can't you think up a better excuse than that?*

Oxford Advanced Learner's Dictionary, 7th edition

6 Decide which other verbs in 4 take an object, then check in your dictionary to see if they are separable or not.

NS How do you write your songs?
David I begin with little ideas that aren't fully formed and I have to either excavate further or enlarge a
45 small idea and turn it into a song – perhaps join it to some other ideas that I have hanging around. So a lot of the time it's more like being a mechanic. **4**☐ I pick up my guitar and within half an hour I've written one. It's an instinctive process, you shut down conscious
50 thought. **5**☐ It's about dredging up things that surprise you: images that you had stored and didn't know you had remembered. One image will unlock a chain of images, and that becomes a song.

NS How do you know if a song is any good?
55 **David** You shouldn't always trust inspiration. Just because it came out of thin air doesn't mean it's any good. **6**☐ The whole feeling, the purity of the germ of the song – it's all so vivid and wondrous. It feels so shockingly fresh. But a song that comes from nowhere
60 is usually much better than anything you consciously think up.

NS What's your state of mind when you're writing?
David It's an extremely intense period. I find myself storming around the room, biting my nails, scratching
65 my head to the point that it bleeds. It's like having an itch you can't scratch until the process is completed. It takes hold of you. That's how you make records. You start off by tinkering around, making a few sounds and having a really good time, but when you
70 get deeper into it and your demands get greater and more ambitious, something rears its ugly head. You become possessed. **7**☐ I find it really hard to get back into normal life.

Vocabulary

Films

1 Look at the list of film types below and think of one example of each type.

a action	h historical drama
b adventure	i musical
c animation	j romantic comedy
d comedy	k science-fiction
e crime	l war
f disaster	m western
g horror	

2 Label the adjectives below as a, b or c. Some may fit into more than one category.

a positive   b negative   c neutral

boring	gripping	scary
funny	powerful	terrible
moving	slow	violent
serious		

3 Say which adjectives in 2 you generally associate with the film types in 1.

4 Tell a partner about a film you really liked, and one you didn't like at all. Say what you liked or didn't like about each one using these words.

acting	costumes	ending
locations	music	special effects
plot	stunts	

Grammar

Simple and continuous tenses
GR p163–164

1 Name the tenses in italics in a–k and choose the correct one to complete each sentence.

a Yesterday evening, we *were having/had* dinner and watched a film on television.

b I don't usually like desserts, but this ice-cream *is tasting/tastes* wonderful.

c The sun *was rising/rose* by the time they finally got to bed.

d Our team *are playing/play* well, but the score is still 0–0.

e Your face is red. *Have you been sitting/Have you sat* in the sun?

f Since his first film in 1984, Johnny Depp *has been playing/has played* many different roles.

g This time next week, I'*ll be sitting/sit* on a beach in the Caribbean.

h It's a good story, but I'*m not believing/don't believe* that it's true!

i Can we stop for a while? We'*ve been walking/'ve walked* since 10 o'clock this morning!

j If you don't study hard for these exams, you'*ll be regretting/'ll regret* it.

k I *always leave/I'm always leaving* my keys at home. I'm so forgetful.

2 Read quotations a–e and correct any continuous forms which should be simple forms, as in the example.

Example   'I̶'̶m̶ ̶t̶h̶i̶n̶k̶i̶n̶g̶ *I think* a pillow should be the peace symbol, not the dove. The pillow has more feathers than the dove, and it isn't having a beak to peck you with.'

a Everywhere is within walking distance if you're having the time.

b I'm remembering when the candle shop burned down. Everyone was standing around singing 'Happy Birthday'.

c I've had a poor memory for as long as I'm remembering.

d I bought a new Japanese car. When I turn on the radio, I'm not understanding a word they're saying.

e There are two types of people in this world, good and bad. The good are sleeping better, but the bad are seeming to enjoy the waking hours much more.

3 Compare these pairs of sentences and explain the difference in meaning between the verbs in italic.

a I *don't see* why you can't help me with my homework.

They *aren't seeing* each other – they're just good friends.

b What *do you think* of Tarantino's latest film?

We'*re thinking* of going to the cinema tomorrow night.

c Our teacher *feels* that we're working harder this year.

We'*re feeling* optimistic about the exam.

d You smile a lot when you *have* a baby.

You don't smile much when you'*re having* a baby.

4 Complete the dialogue by putting the verbs in brackets into the correct tense (future, present or present perfect, simple or continuous).

Joanna You _____ ¹ (sit) on that sofa since lunch-time. What _____ you _____ ² (do)?

Wesley A crossword.

Joanna You _____ ³ (always do) crosswords!

Wesley Well, I _____ ⁴ (enjoy) them. Anyway, I _____ ⁵ (finish) it soon, if you _____ ⁶ (let) me concentrate!

Joanna I _____ ⁷ (never like) crosswords.

Wesley Sshhh! I _____ ⁸ (think)! Four across, 'get better' …

Joanna 'Improve'. Seems pretty easy to me.

Wesley They aren't all that easy. I _____ ⁹ (have) trouble with some of them. For example, can you think of a word that _____ ¹⁰ (mean) 'magnificent'?

Joanna 'Wonderful'?

Wesley No, it _____ ¹¹ (not fit). Eight letters.

Joanna Oh, I _____ ¹² (know). It's 'splendid'.

Wesley Whatabout this one – a small insect that _____ ¹³ (bite)?

Joanna A mosquito?

Wesley That's it! I _____ ¹⁴ (do) it!

5 Complete questions a–e with an appropriate verb and tense (simple or continuous). Then discuss the questions in pairs.

a What _____ you _____ this evening?

b How long _____ you _____ English?

c What _____ you usually _____ on Saturday evenings?

d Where do you think you _____ in ten years' time?

e What _____ you _____ when the teacher came into the room?

Listening

Part 1 Multiple choice

how to do it

Read the question and options carefully as you hear them. Decide what kind of information you are listening for.

In the exam the seven situations are unconnected, so mark your answer after the first listening then concentrate on the next question.

Check your answer during the second listening. If you aren't sure, make a guess.

1 ◉》 Read the **how to do it** box and the example question below, including the three options. Then listen and mark your answer. Say which words helped you decide.

Example   You hear two people discussing ideas for a party.

   Where are they?

   A   in a café

   B   at work

   C   at home

2 ◉》 Listen to people talking in seven different situations and choose the best answers.

1   You hear an actor and a director rehearsing a Shakespeare play.

   What problem did the actor have?

   A   He wasn't speaking loudly enough.

   B   He wasn't putting enough emotion into the lines.

   C   He was standing in the wrong place.

2   You hear a book review on the radio.

   Why doesn't the presenter like the ending of the book?

   A   It's unrealistic.

   B   It's boring.

   C   It's too depressing.

3   You overhear a conversation between a daughter and a parent.

   What agreement do they come to?

   A   She can stay out late if she does her homework now.

   B   If she comes home early, she can finish her homework tomorrow.

   C   If she stays out late, she must finish her homework in the morning.

4   You hear someone talking about their favourite holiday destination.

   What do they like most about it?

   A   the peace and quiet

   B   the friendliness of the people

   C   the scenery

5   You hear a musician talking about songwriting.

   What is she doing?

   A   describing how she writes songs

   B   offering advice on how to write songs

   C   saying why she writes songs about other people

6   You hear an art critic talking on the radio about a painting.

   Why are most people so interested in it?

   A   It's really beautiful.

   B   It was mentioned in a book.

   C   It's been restored.

7   You overhear a conversation in which people are talking about things they'd like to invent.

   Which invention does everybody agree on?

   A   a self-loading dishwasher

   B   a car that parks itself

   C   something that can take the dog for a walk

Speaking

Part 2

1 Look at photo 1 and decide which parts of the picture are real, and which are drawn.

2 Match each of a–i with photos 1 or 2.

a spray paint
b building
c graffiti
d pavement art
e temporary
f chalk
g illusion
h permanent
i shadow

3 In pairs, decide what the two photos have in common. Use these words and your own ideas.

colourful	free	three-dimensional
outdoors	large-scale	urban

4 In pairs, say what is different about the street art in the photos. Talk about

a what exactly the people have drawn or written
b why they may have done it
c what they used (paint, chalk, etc.) and how easy it might be to remove
d how good it is

5 Discuss whether graffiti is vandalism or art. Give reasons for your opinions.

Use of English

Part 2 Open cloze

1 Read the rules about articles in the Grammar Reference (page 163) then match each underlined word or phrase in a–j below with one of the rules.

  a He swam across <u>the English Channel</u> and climbed <u>Ben Nevis</u>, the highest mountain in <u>Britain</u>, in the same week. That's <u>an amazing achievement</u>.

  b <u>After Easter</u> I'll be spending most of my time <u>at home</u>.

  c I've got <u>a cat</u> and <u>a dog</u>. <u>The cat</u> is called Freddie and <u>the dog</u> is called Buster.

  d Thomas Edison was <u>a</u> great scientist and inventor.

  e <u>The British</u> have a reputation for being reserved.

  f The longest river in <u>the world</u> is <u>the Amazon</u>.

  g I always listen to <u>the radio</u> in <u>the morning</u>.

  h I can't stand <u>modern art</u>.

  i <u>After dinner</u> Kate played some tunes on <u>the piano</u>.

  j John lives in <u>Nice</u>, <u>a city</u> on <u>the south coast</u> of <u>France</u>.

2 Quickly read the text below and find

  a the name of the artist
  b the name of two of his famous paintings
  c two things he designed.

3 Read the text again carefully. Then read the **tip** box and complete gaps 1–12 with one word each.

4 Explain the use or non-use of articles in these phrases from the text.

  a a man (l. 1)
  b at school (l. 6)
  c the Duke (l. 15)
  d to France (l. 18)
  e the world (l. 20)
  f the most famous (l. 21)

 tip In this text, gaps 1, 2 and 8 need an article.

RENAISSANCE MAN

LEONARDO DA VINCI was a man before his time, and (0) <u>was</u> considered to be a genius. He became renowned for his multiple talents: he was (1) _____ painter, architect, engineer, mathematician and inventor.

5 He was born in Vinci, outside (2) _____ northern Italian city of Florence, in 1452. While he was at school, his teachers quickly noticed his curiosity and his inquiring mind, even going so far as to complain (3) _____ his endless questions. (4) _____ a youngster, he (5) _____ also discovered to have
10 a talent for drawing. On reaching his fourteenth birthday, Leonardo was apprenticed to Verrochio, a master painter and sculptor, (6) _____ studios and workshops were in the city of Florence. At the age of twenty-six he became his own master, and four years (7) _____ , moved to Milan to work
15 for the Duke there. He travelled between Florence and Milan for most of his life, starting many paintings and sculptures but often not completing them. In his last years he moved to France, where he died in 1519, at (8) _____ age of 67.

He is widely regarded as (9) _____ of the greatest painters
20 in the world. Two of his paintings, *The Last Supper*, and the *Mona Lisa* occupy positions as the most famous, most reproduced and most copied artworks of all time.

As an engineer and inventor, he was ahead (10) _____ his time. Only long after he died (11) _____ people realise how
25 advanced he had been in his thinking. He drew up designs for machines that would only be invented centuries after his death, (12) _____ as a helicopter, a calculator, and a tank.

Vocabulary

Phrasal verbs with *take*

,take sb↔'back to allow sb, such as your husband, wife or partner, to come home after they have left because of a problem ,take sb 'back (to ...) to make sb remember sth: *The smell of the sea took him back to his childhood.* ,take sth↔'back 1 if you take sth back to a shop/store, or a shop/store takes sth back, you return sth that you have bought there, for example because it is the wrong size or does not work 2 to admit that sth you said was wrong or that you should not have said it: *OK, I take it all back!*

Oxford Advanced Learner's Dictionary, 7th edition

1 Read the dictionary entry for *take back* and match each sentence with one of the meanings.

   a This dress is too big. I'll have to take it back.

   b I don't know why she's agreed to take him back after he walked out on her like that.

   c He accused me of lying, but he later took it back and apologised.

   d That song takes me back to my time at college.

tip Phrasal verbs often have more than one meaning. Use the context to help you, then check your ideas in a dictionary.

2 Complete each pair of sentences with one of these words to form phrasal verbs.

apart	in	off	on	up

   a I tried to listen as he gave me the bad news, but I couldn't take .... what he was saying.
   He lost a lot of money when he was taken .... by an email claiming to be from a charity.

   b We collapsed in laughter when Fred took .... the headmaster.
   Mobile phones really took .... in the 1990s.

   c The company has relocated to New York and taken .... 20 new staff.
   Jeff has taken .... far too much work this year and has almost no free time.

   d We'll have to take the wardrobe .... before we try to move it downstairs.
   Italy took France .... in the football final, beating them 4–0.

   e Ian plays the piano beautifully, but he didn't take it .... until he was in his forties.
   The sleeves on this jacket are too long. Can you take them .... for me?

3 Match these verbs and phrases with the meanings of the phrasal verbs in 2.

   a agree to do   f employ
   b become successful   g understand
   c deceive   h pretend to be someone
   d take to pieces   i shorten
   e easily beat   j start

Writing

Part 2 A review

1 Discuss these questions in pairs.

  a Who's your favourite actress and actor?

  b What do you like about them?

  c Which, in your opinion, is the best film they've appeared in? Why?

2 Look at the words and phrases in the box below and discuss these questions.

  a Have you seen any *James Bond* films? If so, did you enjoy them? Why/Why not?

  b Which of these words and phrases are typical of *Bond* films? Give examples from particular films.

> special effects   car chases   beautiful actresses
> exotic locations   villains   stunts
> gripping   light-hearted   funny   violent

3 Read the film review opposite and say in which paragraph the writer mentions a–d.

  a aspects of the film they liked

  b their overall opinion and recommendation to see it

  c background detail, i.e. the title, type of film, book it's based on

  d a brief description of the plot

4 What tense is used to describe the story?

5 Complete the gaps in sentences a–h with these words.

> fan   impressed   miss   performances   set
> short   spectacular   stands   tells   worth

  a There are some excellent .... from the leading actors in the latest *Bond* film.

  b *Spider-Man 3* is .... in New York.

  c What particularly .... me about *Dreamgirls* was the acting.

  d If you're a .... of war films, you won't be disappointed. *Flags of our Fathers* is well .... seeing.

  e I've seen a lot of good films, but there's one that .... out from the rest.

  f In ...., *An Inconvenient Truth* is quite simply the best documentary film I've ever seen. You really shouldn't .... it.

  g *United 93* .... the story of what might have happened on the United Airlines Flight on 11th September 2001.

  h The animated film *Cars* is .... to watch because of the amazing special effects.

FILMREVIEW

I'm not a great fan of action films so I wasn't expecting to enjoy Casino Royale. However, I was pleasantly surprised by this action-packed film, which is based on Ian Fleming's very first James Bond book.

The plot centres on a poker game at the famous Casino Royale. 'Le Chiffre', a master criminal, must be beaten in this game in order to destroy his terrorist network. The game is made complicated by Bond becoming attracted to the mysterious government agent, Vesper Lynn.

The acting is first-rate. Daniel Craig's performance as the young Bond is utterly convincing and he is well supported by the rest of the cast. Visually the film is superb, despite the absence of the spectacular special effects that are a hallmark of other Bond films. Particularly impressive to watch is the opening sequence which involves a 'free running' chase.

I was amazed that I liked this film as much as I did, but I put this down to the power of Daniel Craig's acting. I can wholeheartedly recommend this film to almost anybody.

6 Say which sentences in 5 could be used in a film review to

- a introduce the film.
- b describe the story.
- c describe the acting.
- d describe what it looks like.
- e recommend the film.

how to do it

Divide your review into four paragraphs:

1 introduction (basic information, e.g. title, type of film, actors, director)
2 brief outline of the plot using the present simple – but don't give away the ending!
3 why you liked the film (acting? story? music? special effects? etc.)
4 your overall opinion and recommendation to see it.

7 Read the exam task below and the **how to do it** box. Then write a review including language from this section.

You recently saw this notice in a film magazine called *Silver Screen*.

FILMREVIEWS

Have you seen any good films recently? Write a review telling us why you liked it and send it to *Silver Screen Magazine*.

We'll publish the best reviews in next month's issue.

Review

1 Read the definitions and complete the adjectives that can be used to describe films.

a l _ _ _ _ - h _ _ _ _ _ _ (not very serious)

b s _ _ _ _ (frightening)

c p _ _ _ _ _ _ _ (creating a strong impression)

d g _ _ _ _ _ (very exciting and interesting)

2 Complete sentences a–g with phrasal verbs 1–7 in the correct form.

a They had to .... the computer system when a virus infected it.

b Who are those boys that are .... on the corner of the street?

c The interview .... well but then they asked me some questions that I couldn't answer.

d Can you .... your bag? Someone will trip over it if you leave it there.

e I need to .... a good title for my essay. Any suggestions?

f We couldn't get a table at the restaurant so we .... getting a take-away.

g 'If you don't do as I say,' said the wicked witch, 'I'll .... you .... a frog.'

1 end up
2 hang around
3 pick up
4 shut down
5 start off
6 think up
7 turn into

3 Complete the text using *a/an*, *the* or no article.

LENNON and McCARTNEY

John Lennon and Paul McCartney are considered by some to be (1)............ greatest song-writing team of (2)............ past 50 years. They were brought up in (3)............ Liverpool in England in (4)............ 1940s and 50s. While he was still at (5)............ school, Lennon formed (6)............ group called *The Quarrymen*. One day in 1956, (7)............ group were playing at (8)............ church fête when (9)............ talented young musician called Paul McCartney was introduced to John. They began writing (10)............ songs together in 1957. They would sometimes miss (11)............ school and go to Paul's house while his father was at (12)............ work. There they would make up (13)............ tunes on (14)............ piano. It was (15)............ beginning of (16)............ wonderfully creative partnership. In (17)............ following thirteen years they wrote over 100 songs together before *The Beatles* finally split up in 1970.

4 Complete the missing part of the phrasal verbs in sentences a–k. Use each word below twice.

apart	back	in	off	on	up

Example These jeans are a bit too long so I'll have to take them *up*.

a Don't be taken .... by his promises. He never keeps his word.

b The bed is too big to get through the door. Can you give me a hand to take it ....?

c He's great at impersonating people. He can take .... anybody.

d Our new DVD player didn't work so I took it .... to the shop.

e We can't take .... any more people because we haven't got any free office space.

f The smell of the sea always takes me .... to my childhood.

g Don't take .... any more work. You've already got more than you can cope with.

h In the 1950s, rock 'n' roll really took .... in the USA.

i If you're in London, give me a ring and we can take .... a film or a show.

j If you're bored with life, why don't you take .... a new hobby?

k Brazil have a much stronger team than England, so they will probably take them ....

Real or fake?

Lead in

1 Read the questionnaire below, then complete the gaps with these words.

cheated	forgery	honest	lie	own up
pretend	tell	truth	truthfully	

HOW HONEST ARE YOU?

1 You're having dinner at a friend's house. The friend serves a dish that you really don't like, and says 'I hope you like it'. Would you .... to like it?

2 A friend has a new haircut. You think it looks terrible. Your friend asks: 'What do you think of my new hair cut?' Would you answer .... ?

3 A friend has fallen in love with somebody you don't like. Your friend asks you what you think of this person. Would you be .... with your friend?

4 You accidentally crack a valuable ornament at somebody's house. Nobody sees you do it. Would you .... ?

5 You know that a classmate .... in an exam. Your teacher suspects that this is the case, and asks you if you know anything. What would you say?

6 A relative gives you a shirt as a present. You don't like it, so you give it away. The relative then asks you how often you wear the shirt. Would you .... a lie?

7 You buy a ticket for a big football match from a stranger. Later you notice that it's a .... Do you still try to get into the match?

8 You're at a boring party and you decide to leave. The host, who isn't a close friend, asks you why you are leaving. Would you tell the .... ?

9 You and your parents are planning a surprise birthday party for you grandfather this Saturday. Your grandfather asks if you have any plans for the weekend. Would you .... to your grandfather?

2 In pairs, answer the questionnaire together, then discuss your answers, giving reasons.

3 Think about your answers to the questionnaire. Try to summarise your opinions by completing the sentence below, then compare answers.

It is OK to tell a lie if …

Reading

Part 3 Multiple matching

1 In pairs, discuss the meanings of a–h and match words with similar meanings.

   a a con
   b a fraud
   c genuine
   d an impostor
   e pose as
   f legitimate
   g pretend to be
   h a trick

2 You are going to read a text about four impostors. Before you do, think of as many reasons as you can why someone might become an impostor.

3 Read the text opposite to find out if any of the people become impostors for the reasons you thought of in 1.

4 Read the text again carefully and for questions 1–15, choose from the people (A–D). The people may be chosen more than once.

   Which person

   1   deceived people for financial gain?
   2   had to act younger than his real age?
   3   met a member of a royal family?
   4   tried to make people's lives better?
   5   spent some time in prison?
   6   invented a story about an accident?
   7   was not an easy person to get on with?
   8   did not want to stop working?
   9   changed his name several times?
   10 made many public appearances in Europe?
   11 has a role in a film about his life?
   12 was born over 200 years ago?
   13 went to university?
   14 gave advice to businesses on stopping fraud?
   15 was an early environmentalist?

5 Imagine that you could lead somebody else's life for one week. Whose life would you choose and why? What would you do in that week?

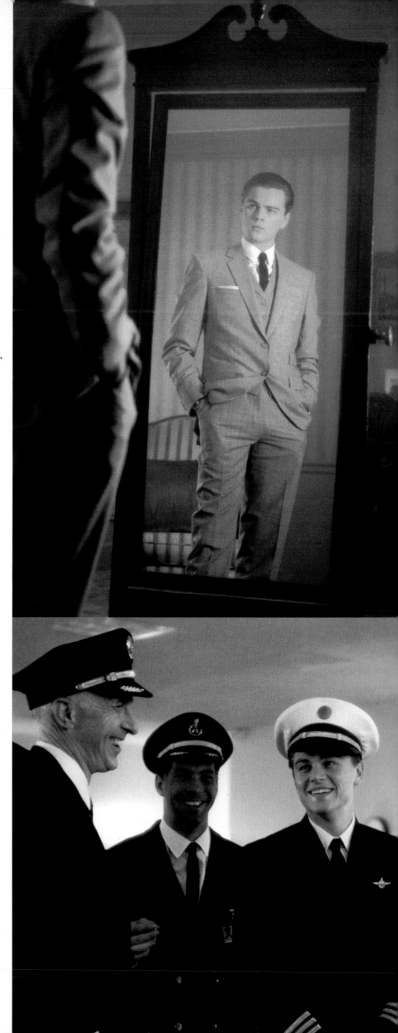

A Doctor James Barry

James Barry was a surgeon in the British Army. Having graduated from Edinburgh University in 1812, he served in India, South Africa and the West Indies. Although he was a difficult and
5 argumentative person who was always getting into trouble with his superiors, Barry worked hard to improve conditions for the troops and for ordinary people wherever he was staying. For example, when he was stationed in Cape
10 Town, South Africa, he developed ways of improving the town's supply of clean water. Barry retired in 1864 – apparently against his wishes – and returned to England. After his death in 1865, the post-mortem examination
15 revealed that James Barry was in fact a woman. It is not clear why Barry chose to live as a man. Nobody is even sure what Barry's real name was. But one thing is certain: at that time, a woman could not have had a career as an army
20 doctor. Being an impostor allowed Barry to help thousands of people around the world.

B Frédéric Bourdin

The pupils at Jean Monnet College in Pau, south-west France, believed everything that their new 15-year-old classmate, Francisco, told them. He
25 claimed that he had just arrived in France from Spain. He said that he had been an orphan since 2000, when his parents had died in a car crash, and that he had spent three months in a coma after the accident. But it was all a lie. Francisco
30 was in fact a 31-year-old Frenchman called Frédéric Bourdin. The school only realised the truth when one of the teachers saw Bourdin on TV, in a documentary about impostors. The school principal, Claire Chardourne, said that the pupil
35 had appeared a bit older than his classmates but she also said that Bourdin had played the part of a 15-year-old brilliantly. 'He told me he had awful scars which he wanted to hide. I gave him special permission to wear a cap. That is how he
40 concealed his true age,' she said. Bourdin has confessed that he loved the attention he could get by pretending to be a youngster. 'In Pau, I got what I wanted. I loved the kids and the people who took care of them. They treated me like one of them.'

C Frank Abagnale

45 In 1964, at the age of 16 Frank Abagnale ran away from home to New York City. He used various cons to get money from banks, changing his identity when they discovered his tricks. For two years he lived as Frank Williams and pretended to be an airline pilot with Pan Am. Wearing a pilot's uniform which he had
50 tricked Pan Am head office into giving him, he used his forged ID card to travel around the world free on Pan Am planes. Later, he changed his name to Frank Conners, moved to Georgia, and posed as a doctor, even though he had no qualifications. When his fiancée realised that he was an impostor, she called the
55 police and Frank had to disappear. But he soon re-emerged with a forged Law Diploma from Harvard University and got a job working for the Attorney General in Louisiana. Over a period of five years, Abagnale used eight different identities and committed fraud in 26 different countries. His luck finally ran out
60 in 1969, when he was arrested in France. After spending several years in jail, Abagnale was released and began a new, legitimate, and very successful career as a consultant to banks on how to prevent fraud. He also wrote a best-selling autobiography which was made into – *Catch Me If You Can* – starring Leonardo
65 DiCaprio and Tom Hanks. Abagnale himself appears briefly in it but, of course, he does not play himself!

IMPOSTORS

D Grey Owl

In 1935, Londoners flocked to see a man called Grey Owl give lectures about the natural world. This unusual character would stand in front of his audience in full North American Indian
70 dress and begin with these words: 'You are tired with years of civilisation. I come to offer you – what? A single green leaf.' Grey Owl was so popular in England that he gave over 200 lectures in four months and addressed 250,000 people about the beauty and significance of the wild. His second lecture tour,
75 in 1937, was an even bigger success – he even gave a private talk to the king of England at Buckingham Palace. What his audiences did not know, however, was that Grey Owl was not a genuine North American Indian at all. In fact, he was not even from North America, but rather from Hastings on the south
80 coast of England, and his real name was Archibald Belaney. As a boy, young Archie had been fascinated by stories of the Canadian wilderness and the life of the people who lived there. So at the age of 18, he left England and went to live and work in Northern Ontario, Canada, where he pretended to be the
85 child of a Scottish father and an Apache mother. It was only after his death that his true identity became public and his reputation suffered badly as a result. But although Grey Owl was a fraud, he did a lot to educate and inspire people about the natural world.

Vocabulary

Verbs connected with speech

1 Check the meaning of these words in a dictionary and put them into two groups: *loud* and *quiet*.

bellow	grumble	mumble	murmur
mutter	scream	shriek	shout	whisper

2 Choose the correct verb for these definitions.

a *bellow/shriek*: to shout in a high voice

b *mutter/whisper*: to speak quietly and unclearly

c *mumble/grumble*: to complain in a quiet voice

d *scream/shout*: to make a loud high cry from fear, pain or excitement

e *murmur/whisper*: to speak using only your breath, not your voice

3 Match sentence halves a–f with 1–6, choosing the correct prepositions.

a He's always *boasting about/for* …

b He finally *confessed to/at* …

c She always *insists in/on* …

d She often *complains about/with* …

e He *objected of/to* …

f He *begged* her *for/with* …

1 the best for her children.

2 another chance to prove his love.

3 his son's fantastic exam results.

4 the way his actions had been reported in the newspaper.

5 breaking my computer.

6 the noise from her neighbour's house.

4 Complete these sentences in an appropriate way.

a '_____,' the teacher grumbled.

b '_____,' the actor boasted.

c '_____,' the police officer insisted.

d '_____,' the photographer begged.

e '_____,' the waiter objected.

f '_____,' the impostor confessed.

g '_____,' the swimmer shrieked.

Grammar

Reported speech GR p168

1 Read the examples of direct speech and reported speech then answer questions a–c below.

1 'I don't want the rest of my pizza,' he insisted.
He insisted <u>that he didn't want the rest of his pizza</u>.

2 'You're standing on my toe,' she told him.
She told him <u>he was standing on her toe</u>.

3 'I'll phone you tomorrow,' she promised him.
She promised <u>that she would phone him the next day</u>.

4 'I only bought these shoes yesterday,' she complained.
She complained <u>that she had only bought the shoes the day before</u>.

a How do the tenses of the verbs change in each pair of sentences?

b How do these types of words change?
   • personal pronouns (I, you, etc.)
   • time expressions (today, tomorrow, etc.)
   • possessive adjectives (my, your, etc.)
   • demonstratives (this, that, etc.)

c Which word sometimes comes at the beginning of the underlined reported speech clauses, but is sometimes omitted?

2 ◀)) Listen to six people, then report what they say using reported speech. Choose the more appropriate of the reporting verbs given.

Example   'I'm trying my hardest!'
          insist   agree
          She insisted that she was trying her hardest.

Speaker 1	promise	warn
Speaker 2	complain	boast
Speaker 3	agree	boast
Speaker 4	beg	explain
Speaker 5	confess	predict
Speaker 6	warn	predict

3 Read reported questions 1–3 then answer a–d below.

1 She asked me where her new shoes were.
2 He asked her what she had done the previous day.
3 She asked them whether they wanted to come back the next day.

a Do reported questions follow the same word order as direct questions?
b Do reported questions use interrogative verb forms?
c What word introduces a reported question when there is no question word? (two possibilities)
d What were the original questions that the people asked?

4 Rewrite the dialogue below as reported speech.

Example Helen asked Mike what he was doing in her bedroom. Mike replied that …

Helen What are you doing in my bedroom?
Mike I'm looking for my mobile phone. Did you borrow it?
Helen I've never borrowed your mobile phone.
Mike You used it yesterday!
Helen I didn't make any calls. I was just looking for a phone number.
Mike Where did you leave it?
Helen I can't remember. Have you looked on the kitchen table?
Mike I've looked everywhere!

5 For a–e rewrite the reported speech with infinitives as direct speech.

a The neighbours asked him not to tell anyone.
   '.. anyone.'
b The police ordered him to put his hands on his head.
   '.. head.'
c His girlfriend told him not to worry about anything.
   '.. anything.'
d Jenny agreed to help him with his homework.
   '.. homework.'
e The managing director advised her to apply for the job.
f '.. job.'
   The kidnappers warned him not to contact the police.
   '.. the police.'

6 In pairs, tell each other about a–d.

a the most difficult thing that you've ever been asked to do
b the most surprising thing that anybody has ever told you
c something that you were always warned not to do as a child
d a promise someone didn't keep

7 Complete the newspaper article with the infinitive or other appropriate form of the verb in brackets. Add pronouns and other words if necessary.

BOBBY MASON was a celebrity in the small village of Southbourne where he lived. His neighbours often asked him ¹............ (tell) stories about his years as a top professional footballer in the 1960s. Bobby entertained them for hours. He told them ²............ (play) against George Best, one of the most famous footballers in the world at that time.

The problem was, it wasn't true. Although Bobby Mason was indeed the name of a footballer from the 1960s, the Bobby Mason in Southbourne had never been a footballer – he'd been a carpenter. When somebody told the real Bobby Mason what ³............ (happen), he was so angry that he drove to Southbourne and ordered the impostor ⁴............ (explain). The impostor admitted that ⁵............ (impersonate) the footballer, but claimed that it ⁶............ (start) by accident. 'People kept asking me if ⁷............ (be) the same Bobby Mason as the footballer. At first, I told them ⁸............ (not be), but when people kept asking, I almost started to believe it was true.'

Listening

Part 4 Multiple choice

1 Read the description opposite of a TV programme called *Faking it*. Which of the identities below do you think a female singer in a choir might be asked to take?

> a fashion photographer   a racing driver
> a rock singer   a television director

2 •))) Listen to an account of choirgirl Laura-Jane Foley's experiences in *Faking it* and answer these questions.

  a Did you guess correctly in 1?

  b Did Laura-Jane 'fake it' successfully?

3 •))) Listen again and choose the best answer for 1–7.

  1 How did Laura-Jane and the programme-makers first make contact?

    A The programme-makers emailed lots of choir singers, including Laura-Jane.

    B Laura-Jane phoned the TV company.

    C The programme-makers went to see her choir.

  2 Laura-Jane was amazed that

    A the programme-makers were interested in a Cambridge student.

    B so many people from the TV company went to see her.

    C the programme-makers started filming so soon.

  3 Laura-Jane's new identity was going to be

    A BJ, lead singer of the band *Remake*.

    B JJ, lead singer of the band *Reload*.

    C LJ, lead singer of the band *Rehab*.

  4 According to Laura-Jane, why were arguments with Harry inevitable?

    A Harry leads a real rock singer's lifestyle.

    B Harry and Laura-Jane both have strong opinions.

    C They only had four weeks for all the training.

  5 Laura-Jane thought her first rock concert

    A was not very safe.

    B was frightening but fun.

    C was fun, but not something she'd want to do again.

  6 In what sense was Laura-Jane's training a failure?

    A She didn't really change her style or attitude.

    B She didn't enjoy the whole experience of becoming a rock singer.

    C She didn't make the judges believe that she was a real rock singer.

  7 One positive result of the experience is that it made Laura-Jane

    A change her views on life.

    B become a more confident person.

    C change her opinion of rock singers.

4 Look at the challenges in 1 again and discuss in pairs which one you would most like to try. Say why, and how successful you think you would be.

Faking it **is a TV show which challenges people to adopt a completely new identity. Can they learn the new skills, style and attitude so well that, at the end of the four weeks, even experts do not realise that they're faking it? There is always a big contrast between each person's real life and the new identity that they are asked to adopt. For example, in one programme, a quiet, shy chess player had to become the manager of a football team. And in another, a singer in a punk rock band became the conductor of a classical orchestra. The interesting part of the show is not only whether they manage to fool the experts, but also what they learn about themselves as people.**

Speaking

Part 1

1 Read questions a–f below and in pairs brainstorm some ideas and words you might use to answer them.

   a What's your ideal holiday destination and why?

   b Are you a fan of new technology? Why/Why not?

   c Do you enjoy eating out? (Why/Why not?)

   d Do you judge people by the way they dress?

   e Tell me about something that went wrong for you recently.

   f What are your earliest memories?

2 ◉)) Listen to five people answering questions from 1 and answer a–c.

   a Which question was not answered?

   b Did you hear any of the words from your list?

   c What other words gave away which question the speaker was answering?

3 ◉)) Listen again. Match each speaker from 2 to two of the phrases below, one from each language box.

••● Allowing your self time to think

Speaker	
....	I need to think for a moment.
....	That's an interesting question.
....	Well, it's difficult to say, really.
....	Let me see.
....	It depends what you mean, exactly.

••● Introducing your answer

Speaker	
....	I guess the honest answer would be …
....	I suppose the simplest answer to that question is …
....	If I think about it, I suppose …
....	It's hard to generalise, but on balance …
....	The best example that comes to mind is …

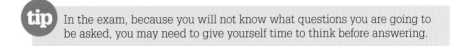

tip In the exam, because you will not know what questions you are going to be asked, you may need to give yourself time to think before answering.

4 Work in pairs as Student A and B and do the following.

- Student A ask B three of the questions from 1 and pay attention to the answers.
- Student B answer two of A's question honestly, but invent the answer to the other. Try to include phrases from 3 in your answers.
- Student A try to guess which of Student B's answers was invented.
- Swap roles so that Student B asks three questions.

Use of English

Part 3 Word formation

●●● Negative prefixes

Common negative prefixes in English are *un–*, *in–*, (*im–*, *il–*, *ir –*) and *dis–*. They can be added to certain verbs, but more often to adjectives and adverbs.

wrap – unwrap
aware – unaware
practical – impractical
appear – disappear
honestly – dishonestly

1 Read the information about negative prefixes. Then add negative prefixes to a–g, checking in a dictionary if necessary.

a active
b allow
c legal
d injured
e possible
f sane
g sympathetically

2 Choose the correct word from those you formed in 1 to complete these sentences.

a 'Stop crying and go home,' she said _____ .
b He was lucky to escape from the accident _____ .
c In many countries it's _____ to drive a car without wearing a seatbelt.
d Why did the referee _____ that goal? It looked OK to me!
e According to Einstein, it's _____ to travel faster than the speed of light.
f The volcano had been _____ for hundreds of years before it erupted.
g You'd have to be _____ to swim in that water – it's full of sharks!

3 Read the text opposite, ignoring the gaps, to find out what the two characters in the pictures have in common.

4 Read the **how to do it** box. Then read the text again carefully and complete gaps 1–10 with words formed from those below.

0	distinguish	6	real
1	possible	7	technology
2	aware	8	likely
3	act	9	appear
4	practical	10	questionable
5	immediate		

● how to do it

Read the text once, ignoring the gaps, to find out what it is about.

Look at the context of each missing word and work out what part of speech it must be.

Find a word related to the base word which is the correct part of speech.

Read your completed text to check that it makes sense.

5 Does it matter whether you are watching a real actor or a computer-generated actor, if you can't tell the difference? Why/Why not?

Vocabulary

Idioms connected with speech

1 Match expressions a–h with definitions 1–8.

  a speak out against something
  b speak your mind
  c get to the point
  d get the wrong end of the stick
  e talk about someone behind their back
  f talk down to someone
  g talk someone into (doing) something
  h talk someone out of (doing) something

  1 say bad things about someone without them knowing
  2 say publicly that something is bad
  3 persuade someone not to do something
  4 talk to someone as if they are not very intelligent
  5 persuade someone to do something
  6 misunderstand
  7 say exactly what you think
  8 begin the most important part of what you want to say

2 Complete sentences a–h with the correct form of the expressions in 1.

  a She's a politician who .... all forms of injustice.
  b Even though we were teenagers, some teachers still .... us, as if we were young children.
  c My aunt insisted on taking three suitcases on holiday, even though we tried to .... it.
  d My cousin took fifteen minutes to .... , and ask to borrow some money.
  e I think you've .... – I only want to have dinner at this hotel, I don't need a room.
  f Tanya was upset to find out that two of her best friends had been ....
  g At first I didn't want to go skiing, but in the end my friends .... it.
  h My dad is very direct. He always .... , even if it offends people from time to time.

COMPUTER-GENERATED IMAGES are now so lifelike that, in photos at least, they are almost **0** *indistinguishable* from the real world. Although it is more challenging to produce computer-generated video images that are **1** .... to tell apart from real videos, the technology is improving rapidly. When audiences around the world watched the film *Titanic*, most of them were probably **2** .... that many of the actors were not human. The people jumping or falling from the ship as it sinks are in fact computer-generated **3** .... – or 'synthespians', as they are sometimes known. It would have been **4** .... , and extremely dangerous, to use real actors for these scenes. The film *Gladiator* also uses synthespians for some spectacular crowd scenes which would have been impossible with real actors. Of course, in both of these films, we do not see close-up shots of the computer-generated characters because it would have been **5** .... obvious that they were not real. More recent films have included computer-generated actors as main characters (for example, Gollum in *The Lord of the Rings*), or even characters who are a mix of real and computer-generated images, such as Davy Jones in *Pirates of the Caribbean 2*. A **6** .... human face is the most difficult challenge, but with the speed of **7** .... progress, it seems probable that this will be achieved soon. However, it is **8** .... that the rise of computer-generated characters will ever cause human actors to **9** .... completely. Who would become a fan of an actor who did not exist in the real world? But their **10** .... benefits when it comes to fantasy characters, stunts and crowd scenes, surely mean that synthespians are here to stay.

Writing

Part 2 An essay

1 Read the model question and essay below, then explain the term 'white lie' in your own words.

2 Choose the correct verbs to complete these common expressions, then check your answers by finding them in the essay in 1.

a to *say/tell* a lie

b to *say/tell* the truth

c to *damage/hurt* somebody's feelings

d to *feel/sense* guilty

e when it *comes/goes* to important matters

You have had a class discussion about honesty. Your teacher has asked you to write an essay with the title: *Is honesty always the best policy?* Write your essay in 120–180 words.

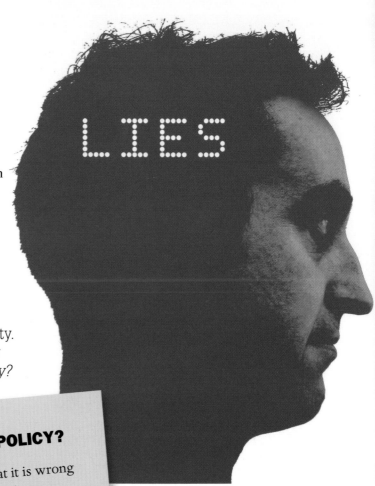

IS HONESTY ALWAYS THE BEST POLICY?

We teach our children from a young age that it is wrong to tell a lie. However, as adults we often find that we need to avoid telling the truth to avoid hurting somebody's feelings.

Small lies (or 'white lies') to protect other people's feelings are an everyday part of life. When friends ask for your opinion, they sometimes want reassurance, not honest criticism. 'Do you like my new coat?' requires a positive answer, even if you hate the coat. Most people tell white lies like this all the time, without feeling guilty or immoral.

It is true that there are people who refuse to lie, even if telling the truth is unpopular. These people always speak their mind, no matter how insensitive other people might find them. Their friends usually accept this as part of their personality, and may even admire it.

In conclusion, I believe that for most of us, honesty is the best policy when it comes to important matters. However, white lies are a frequent and necessary part of our social life.

3 In pairs, brainstorm ideas for an essay with the same title as the one in the model. Use these ideas to help you.

a attitudes towards lying and honesty: schools, parents, the law

b situations when you might lie to protect somebody's feelings

c situations when you might lie for other reasons (e.g. to avoid an argument)

d situations when you should tell the truth, whatever the consequences

e possible negative consequences of 'white lies'

f your personal conclusion

4 Divide the ideas in 3 into four paragraphs, following the same pattern as in the model.

- paragraph 1   a few introductory ideas
- paragraph 2   examples of when honesty may not always be the best policy
- paragraph 3   examples that support the opposite side of the argument
- paragraph 4   a personal opinion to sum up

5 Decide in which paragraph or paragraphs of your essay you might be able to use each of phrases a–k.

a To sum up, …

b In addition, …

c In conclusion, …

d To begin with, it is important to …

e On the other hand, …

f Firstly, it is worth considering …

g I'd like to begin by …

h Furthermore, …

i To summarise, then …

j However, it could be argued that …

k An example of this would be …

6 Read the phrases in the language box below and find one which is used in the model answer.

Introducing facts and opinions

People often find that …
Some people believe that … but others insist …
It is true that …
It is often said that …
Nobody could deny that …
It is sometimes suggested that …

tip When giving different points of view, avoid using *I*; instead use impersonal phrases like the ones in the language box.

7 Use the phrases in the language box to introduce some of the ideas you brainstormed in 3.

Example   It's sometimes suggested that it's unacceptable to lie to a police officer.

8 Write your answer to the essay question in 1. Use your ideas and paragraph plan from 3 and 4, and useful phrases from 5 and 6.

Review

1 Complete sentences a–f with the most appropriate of these verbs.

begged	boasted	confessed	insisted
shouted	whispered		

a 'I'm earning five times as much as my brother,' he _____ .

b 'I'm afraid I've lost those keys,' he _____ .

c 'I've seen this film before,' she _____ in his ear.

d 'My car is on fire!' she _____ .

e 'Please, please, stop singing!' he _____ .

f 'I really will be on time tomorrow,' he _____ .

2 Rewrite the sentences in 1 as reported speech.

3 Add negative prefixes to these words.

a _____ civilised   e _____ sincere

b _____ accurate   f _____ grateful

c _____ logical   g _____ tolerant

d _____ probable   h _____ loyal

4 Use the words from 3, with or without the negative prefix, to complete these sentences.

a I'm very _____ for the help you have given me.

b The earliest attempts to measure the size of the Earth were surprisingly _____ , given the lack of scientific instruments available at the time.

c My parents are very _____ – they don't let me play loud music!

d That dog was a _____ friend to me for 15 years.

e It's _____ to choose to go on a cruise to the Arctic and then complain about the cold weather.

f I believed everything you told me because I thought you were _____ .

g It's rather _____ to wipe your nose on your sleeve.

h Cars are a _____ cause of climate change.

5 Complete sentences a–e with an appropriate word.

a I'm going bungee jumping and nobody is going to talk me _____ of it.

b Martin Luther King Jr spoke _____ against racism.

c I think I've got the wrong _____ of the stick. I thought you wanted to go out tonight?

d Please get to the _____ – I haven't got all day!

e Have you talked your parents _____ paying for your holiday?

6 Read the text and complete gaps 1–10 with words formed from those below.

0 discover
1 collect
2 examine
3 appear
4 connect
5 believable
6 follow
7 science
8 care
9 old
10 honest

IN 1912, a scientific (0) _discovery_ made newspaper headlines around the world. An amateur fossil (1) _____ called Charles Dawson took a 500,000-year-old skull to a museum. After a thorough (2) _____ of the skull, the scientists told Dawson that it belonged to a kind of ape that had (3) _____ from the Earth thousands of years earlier. It represented a missing (4) _____ between modern humans and their ape ancestors. It was an (5) _____ important piece of the jigsaw and became known as 'Piltdown Man'.

Dawson told the scientists that he intended to collect more fossils from the same location. Over the (6) _____ few years, he took other bones to the museum and the scientists gave Piltdown Man a (7) _____ name: Eoanthropus dawson.

However, in 1953, three scientists from the British museum re-examined the bones (8) _____ and uncovered the truth: the bones were a mixture of human and animal bones. They had been covered in a special substance to make them look (9) _____ than they really were. Piltdown Man was a fake and Charles Dawson had been (10) _____ about the fossils from the beginning!

Journeys

Lead in

1 Look at the photos. Say whether or not you would enjoy these ways of travelling. Give reasons, thinking about the following and your own ideas.

- scenery
- comfort
- speed
- company

2 In pairs think of as many reasons as you can why people go on holiday. Discuss your ideas with another pair.

3 In many countries people are taking longer, more frequent and more expensive holidays than in previous generations. Why do you think this is? Think about

- work and pay
- the Internet
- cost of travel
- lifestyles and interests

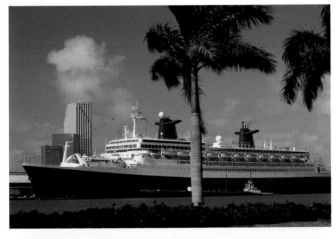

Reading

Part 1 Multiple choice

Slovenian man's 5,265 km Amazon swim

Across the USA on a lawnmower

British women reach North and South Poles on foot

1 Read the newspaper headlines opposite. Discuss what problems these people might have faced on their journeys, and which you think was most difficult.

2 Read the text opposite quickly to find out what journey David Cornthwaite made. Think of a possible newspaper headline to describe it.

3 Match adjectives a–e with nouns 1–5, then check your answers in the text, and explain what the phrases mean.

a	epic	1	lorry
b	articulated	2	vehicle
c	constant	3	journey
d	four-wheel drive	4	speech
e	motivational	5	pain

4 Read the text again carefully and choose the best answers for 1–8.

1 Why did David Cornthwaite decide to skateboard across Australia?
   - A He was an experienced skateboarder.
   - B He wanted to break a world record.
   - C He was bored with his life and wanted to try something different.
   - D Somebody gave him a guidebook about Australia.

2 His preparation in Britain was
   - A successful, but painful.
   - B successful, but more time-consuming than planned.
   - C successful, but more difficult than he had realised.
   - D unsuccessful because he got injured.

3 What made David fall off his skateboard several times in Australia?
   - A thunderstorms in the Outback
   - B the trains that race across the Outback
   - C the injuries on his feet
   - D the wind created by huge lorries going past

4 At times, David felt as though he
   - A needed to stop for a while.
   - B wanted to give up completely.
   - C wanted to get out of the sun.
   - D needed a new pair of shoes.

5 During the journey, where did David sleep at night?
   - A in a four-wheel drive vehicle
   - B in a tent
   - C outdoors on the Nullarbor Plain
   - D in the homes of his supporters

6 David fell off his skateboard because
   - A he was going too fast.
   - B he was exhausted and in pain.
   - C he didn't see a hole in the road.
   - D he was thinking about finishing his journey.

7 Why does David think surfing is a good thing to do after his journey?
   - A He can stay close to Brisbane.
   - B He's always wanted to surf on the Gold Coast.
   - C He wants to strengthen the top half of his body.
   - D He needs to keep his legs strong.

8 What does David hope to do eventually?
   - A encourage other people to feel more positive about themselves
   - B put his skateboard away
   - C return to work as a designer
   - D persuade other people to make long-distance journeys

5 Work in pairs. Role-play an interview with one of the people from the headlines in 1. Include these questions and add your own ideas.

a 'How do you feel, now that you've finished your epic journey?'

b 'What were the worst moments along the way?'

c 'Have you got any similar treks in mind for the future?'

COAST TO COAST

A 27-year-old graphic designer from Oxfordshire in England completed a record-breaking journey across Australia yesterday. It was a 5,800 kilometre odyssey – and he travelled the whole distance on a skateboard. David Cornthwaite, who started skateboarding less than two years ago, decided on his epic journey after waking up one morning and realising he hated his job. 'I thought, the only thing keeping me going is the skate to and from work. I was a bit disillusioned and I was looking for something new,' he said. 'I saw a Lonely Planet guide to Australia. There was a map on the back. Perth was on one side and Brisbane on the other and I thought, "that'll do".'

He decided to prepare by skateboarding from John O'Groats to Lands End: the two points furthest apart on the British mainland. That 1,442 kilometre trek, which he finished in June, took just over a month, during which an infected blister swelled to the 'size of a tennis ball'.

Crossing Australia on a skateboard brought unique challenges. The wind caused by huge road trains, the articulated lorries that thunder across the Outback, was so powerful that he was sometimes blown off his board. Multiple blisters and aching ankles, toes and feet, have kept him in almost constant pain for the last six weeks. 'I feel like an old man. I'm not sure that anyone has ever had this many blisters,' he said. Temperatures of 40°C and above mean that he has used more than a dozen tubes of factor 30 sunscreen. 'There have been moments where I thought "this is ridiculous, I have to rest", but I never contemplated giving up.' He has worn through 13 pair of shoes and has an over-developed right calf muscle which he compares to 'a giant chicken fillet'.

Skating an average of 50 kilometres a day and hitting speeds of up to 50kph on downhill runs, he left Perth, Western Australia, and skated across the fearsome Nullarbor Plain into South Australia. After reaching Adelaide he made his way to Melbourne and from there to Sydney. A support team of seven people trailed him all the way in a four-wheel drive vehicle, which included camping equipment for night stops. The journey has smashed the previous record for a long-distance skateboard, set by an American, Jack Smith, who covered 4,800 kilometres across the US in 2003.

David Cornthwaite was less than three kilometres from the end of his epic journey when he hit a hole and was thrown off his skateboard, suffering cuts and bruises to his shoulders, knees, hips and elbows. 'I was only going at 40km at the time, so although it wasn't pretty, but it could have been a lot worse,' he said.

In the short term, he hopes to spend the next few days surfing on the Gold Coast, south of Brisbane, to build up some much-needed upper body strength. 'I've got huge legs but a skinny body – it's a bit ridiculous. I need to give my body a chance to warm down and surfing sounds ideal. For the time being I'm hanging up my skateboard.' In the longer term, he plans to give motivational speeches and write a book. Another long-distance journey is also on the cards. 'I'm certainly not going back to the day job,' he said.

Vocabulary

Travel

1 Decide which word in each of a–f does not belong. Say what connects the other three words.

  a platform check-in departure lounge customs

  b hand luggage baggage overhead locker suitcase

  c sail wing cabin mast

  d bus driver flight attendant ticket inspector propeller

  e barge ferry hovercraft scooter

  f passport ticket ticket office visa

2 Choose the correct verb in phrases a–f.

  a *to board/to mount* a plane

  b *to lift/to pick up* a passenger

  c *to get onto/to get into* a motorbike

  d *to change/to move* trains

  e *to cancel/to take away* a flight

  f *to get onto/to get into* a car

3 Complete the email with words and phrases from 1 and 2 in the correct form.

○ ○ ○   **New Message**   ⊂⊃

☰▼

What a terrible journey!! The taxi was late ⁰ *picking* us ___up___ , so we got to the station two minutes before our train left. There was a queue at the ¹_____ , so we went straight to the ²_____ and got onto the train, which was just about to leave. When we tried to buy a ticket from the ³_____ , we discovered that we were on the wrong train. We had to get off at the next station and ⁴_____ trains, which is a nightmare when you're carrying four large ⁵_____ !

At the airport, we queued for an hour at ⁶_____ to get our boarding pass and then we waited in the ⁷_____ for two hours become being called to the gate. When they finally allowed us to ⁸_____ the plane, I found that I'd been given a window seat, even though I'd asked for an aisle seat. And to cap it all, the plane sat on the runway for fifty minutes because of a technical problem.

The end of the flight was just as bad. We landed with a huge bump, the ⁹_____ above my seat flew open, and my own ¹⁰_____ fell down and hit me on the shoulder.

Grammar

Modal verbs: advice, ability, prohibition and obligation
GR p169–170

1 Choose the correct modal verb in sentences a–g.

  a 'You really *could/must* go to the Picasso museum while you're in Barcelona – it's fantastic!'

  b 'I don't think you *should/must* take the car. The shops are only a few hundred metres away!'

  c You *can't/mustn't* lose your boarding pass. You *can't/mustn't* board the plane without it.

  d I think you *ought to/may* go by train – it's much faster than the coach.

  e Martin *should/could* see the train pulling away from the platform, but he *can't/couldn't* reach it in time.

  f You *can't/mustn't* drive when you're tired. It's dangerous.

  g To avoid risk of injury, passengers *must/may* remain seated during take-off and landing.

2 Read the sentences in 1 again and answer questions a–c.

  a Which three different modals can we use for giving advice, and which is the most emphatic?

  b Which modal do we use for obligation in its affirmative form, and prohibition in its negative form?

  c Which modal do we use to talk about ability in the past and what is its present tense form?

3 Work in pairs, Student A and Student B. Take it in turns to listen to your partner's problems and give advice, using a variety of appropriate modal verbs. Use the ideas below or your own.

A's problems
- need to improve English – new job three months' time
- argued with friend – won't answer phone calls
- headaches every evening, especially using computer or TV

B's problems
- interview next week – don't know anything about company
- friend's birthday – haven't got any money
- fancy dress party – Hollywood theme – can't think what to wear

4 Read the **tip** box. Then find and correct two examples in the text where *could* should be *managed to*.

I stood on the beach and waved my arms, shouting. Eventually, I could attract Harry's attention and he steered the boat in our direction. He couldn't come too close to the beach in case the boat became grounded, so we waded out to meet it. The waves were quite strong, and I could see that Jacqui was nervous. I remembered that Mark could swim, but Jacqui couldn't. I held her arm as the water became deeper. When the boat came alongside, I could grab hold of the ladder and hold it steady while she climbed aboard.

5 Complete sentences a–f with *must, mustn't, have/has to* or *don't have to*.

a You .... park there. It's for emergency vehicles only.

b You .... wear your seatbelt during the whole flight, but it's advisable to keep it fastened while you're in your seat.

c Please note that all passengers .... check in at least 45 minutes before the scheduled departure time.

d There's no bus into town, so I always .... walk or cycle.

e People over 65 .... pay to travel by bus – it's free.

f These days, you .... smoke on any flight.

6 Complete the text below using modal verbs in the correct form. More than one answer may be possible.

Greener Travel

You are no doubt aware of the negative impact which international travel has on the environment, but you may not realise how much you ¹ .... do to minimise it. And you ² .... give up travelling altogether – you ³ .... make a difference just by taking a few simple measures.

Your efforts ⁴ .... start even before leaving home. You ⁵ ...... leave TVs, hi-fis and other electrical equipment on standby because that wastes a surprising amount of electricity.

While on holiday, you ⁶ ...... use public transport when available, rather than hiring a car. If you're staying in a hotel, remember that you ⁷ ...... have clean towels every day, you ⁸ .... easily re-use them. And of course, you absolutely ⁹ .... avoid buying souvenirs that are made from endangered species.

Listening

Part 1 Multiple choice

1 **Look at travel problems a–f and decide which forms of transport they could apply to.**

a The crossing was cancelled owing to bad weather.

b We had a flat tyre.

c The driver got lost.

d We ran out of petrol.

e We missed our stop.

f We couldn't find our tickets.

2 **You will hear people talking in eight different situations. Listen, and for questions 1–8 choose the best answer (A, B or C).**

1 You hear two people talking about a party. Where are they?

A in a taxi

B on a bus

C in a car

2 You hear a woman buying a ticket. How many different forms of transport will she need to use for her journey?

A two

B three

C four

3 You hear a man and a woman talking. What are they looking at?

A a ferry

B a big ship

C the sea

4 You hear a man at an airport. What is he doing?

A going through customs

B checking in

C going through passport control

5 You hear a woman talking to a mechanic. What's the problem with her motorbike?

A a damaged wheel and a flat tyre

B a flat tyre and a broken mirror

C a broken mirror and a damaged wheel

6 You hear a man and a woman talking in a car. Why does the woman become angry?

A The man forgot to look at the map.

B The man won't stop the car to ask for directions.

C The traffic warden doesn't help them.

7 You hear a woman talking about her home town. What has made travelling easier for her?

A more taxis

B cheaper bus fares

C cycle lanes

8 You hear a taxi driver talking to a passenger. Why is there no petrol in the taxi?

A There's a problem with the vehicle.

B The driver forgot to fill up with petrol.

C The petrol stations are all closed.

3 **In pairs, take it in turns to find out about your partner's worst travel experience. Use these ideas to help you.**

• where they were going from and to

• what time of year it was

• who they were travelling with

• what form of transport they used

• how long the journey should have taken and how long it actually took

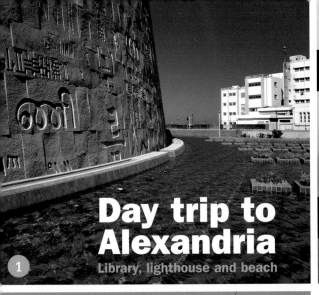

Day trip to Alexandria
Library, lighthouse and beach
1

HELICOPTER TRIP

30-MINUTE FLIGHT OVER THE PYRAMIDS!
2

Nile Adventure
EVENING CRUISE
3

DESERT SAFARI
Two-day camping excursion by jeep
4

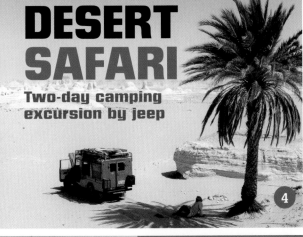

SAQQARA
BY CAMEL

Visit the tombs of the first pharaohs
5

Speaking

Part 3

1 Look at the advertisements for trips and excursions from Cairo. Decide which one
   a probably takes the shortest time.
   b probably involves sleeping in a tent.
   c has the slowest form of transport.
   d may include swimming in the sea.

2 ◉ Listen to five short dialogues and match them with the advertisements. Which words gave you the answers?

3 ◉ Listen again and match two of phrases a–j to each dialogue (1–5).
   a … seems like the best option to me. ☐
   b If you ask me, I really think we should … ☐
   c Personally, I'm in favour of … ☐
   d Believe me, … ☐
   e I'm sure it will be worth it. ☐
   f Let's go for it. ☐
   g … don't you agree? ☐
   h I'm really keen on the idea of … ☐
   i But just think of the … ! ☐
   j Oh, come on! ☐

4 In pairs, use phrases from 3 to talk about how enjoyable you think each excursion might be, and why. Decide which one to go on.

5 Work in pairs, taking turns to be A and B, and do the following.
   Student A: Think of two different excursions that you could go on in your own country or region. Describe them to your partner. Say
   • what you would see
   • how you would travel
   • how long the excursion would last

   Student B: Say which one you would prefer to go on and why.

Use of English

Part 4 Key word transformations

1 For each of a–f, decide which of 1–6 below can replace the words or phrases in bold.

a Please leave your mobile number at reception **so that** we can contact you in an emergency.

b I couldn't remember **if** I'd left my key in my hotel room.

c This room does not look **as if** it has been cleaned.

d The café is open all day, **while** the main restaurant only opens at meal times.

e We may as well have breakfast, **seeing that** it's included in the room rate.

f The hotel has a gymnasium **and** a swimming pool.

1 as though
2 as well as
3 in order that
4 since
5 whereas
6 whether

2 Read the example. Then, for each of a–f, write a sentence with the same meaning. Replace the word in bold with a word or phrase with the opposite meaning, and make any other changes necessary.

Example Her parents won't buy her a car unless she **passes** her driving test.

passes → fails (unless → if)

Her parents won't buy her a car if she fails her driving test.

a Passengers must not **stand** while the coach is moving.

b Phone me if you know that your flight won't be **on time**.

c Travelling by bus is **cheaper** than travelling by taxi.

d The more expensive seats are more **comfortable**.

e When there's a lot of traffic, the journey is **slower**.

f The use of mobile phones is **forbidden** during the flight.

3 Rewrite each sentence a–f keeping the meaning the same. Use two to five words, including the word given.

a If the flight is on time, we should arrive at the hotel before 9pm.
provided
We should get to the hotel by 9pm .... late.

b You might need to get a taxi, so take some money with you.
case
Take some money with you .... to get a taxi.

c This year's holiday was less enjoyable than last year's.
fun
Last year's holiday .... this year's.

d Travellers are not allowed to bring pets into the UK unless they have a 'pet visa'.
only
Travellers can .... into the UK if they have a 'pet visa'.

e The journey was better than I'd expected.
bad
The journey .... as I'd expected.

f That ferry seems to be leaning to one side.
though
That ferry looks .... to one side.

Vocabulary

Idioms with *come* and *go*

1 Choose the correct verb to complete sentences a–h. Use a dictionary to check your answers and make sure you understand the meaning of the phrases in italics.

   a I refused to pay the mechanic's bill in full because the work didn't *come/go up to scratch*.

   b She'd always loved Tom Cruise, so meeting him at the film première was *a dream come/gone true*.

   c *As far as* rooms *come/go*, it was OK, but it was nothing special.

   d *When it comes/goes to* sailing, I know almost nothing.

   e I can get by in French and Spanish, although languages don't *come/go easily to* me.

   f My brother passed his driving test at the sixth attempt, which *just comes/goes to show* that you should never give up!

   g We had a flat tyre just after we set off, and after that, the journey *came/went from bad to worse*.

   h I tried to think of a clever reply, but nothing *came/went to mind*.

2 Read the text below, then rewrite the underlined parts (1-8) using phrases from 1.

As far as holidays are concerned (1) I usually choose something cheap, so you can imagine my surprise when my husband booked a cruise. Compared to most cruise ships (2) ours was not particularly large or luxurious, and we were disappointed that there were no staff to help us with our luggage. The situation got even worse (3) however, when we finally found our accommodation. It was small, badly furnished and dirty. What we thought of first (4) was a prison cell, not a luxury cabin. Like many people, I don't find it easy to complain (5), but on this occasion I had to say something because the accommodation simply wasn't satisfactory (6). Reluctantly, the staff agreed to move us to another, slightly more comfortable cabin, which proves (7) that complaining *can* work. But some of the passengers were heartbroken; they had been looking forward to the holiday of a lifetime, but this cruise was a nightmare rather than a really enjoyable experience (8).

Writing

Part 1 An informal email

1 Read the emails below, and say in what order Maria answers Sonia's questions.

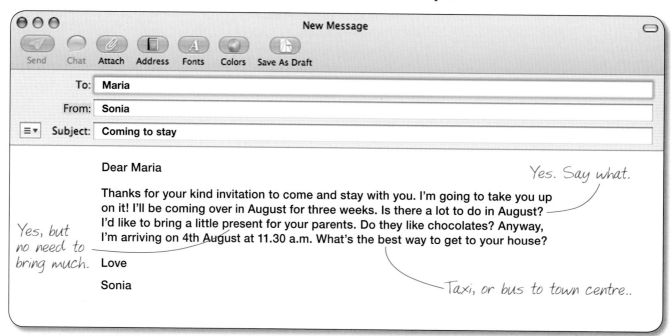

New Message

Send Chat Attach Address Fonts Colors Save As Draft

To: Maria

From: Sonia

Subject: Coming to stay

Dear Maria

Yes, but no need to bring much.

Thanks for your kind invitation to come and stay with you. I'm going to take you up on it! I'll be coming over in August for three weeks. Is there a lot to do in August? — *Yes. Say what.*
I'd like to bring a little present for your parents. Do they like chocolates? Anyway, I'm arriving on 4th August at 11.30 a.m. What's the best way to get to your house?

Love

Sonia

Taxi, or bus to town centre..

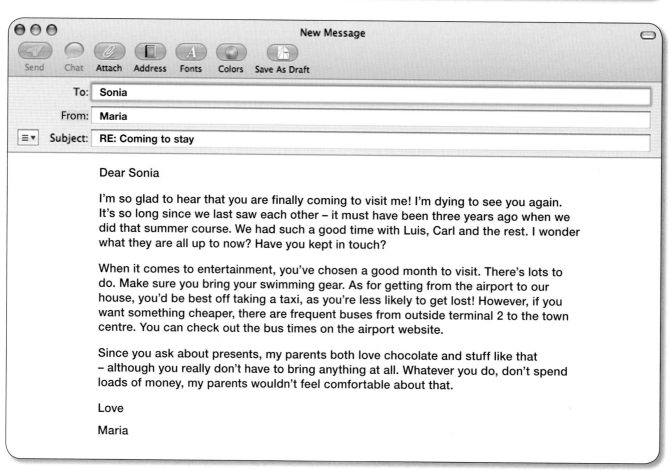

New Message

Send Chat Attach Address Fonts Colors Save As Draft

To: Sonia

From: Maria

Subject: RE: Coming to stay

Dear Sonia

I'm so glad to hear that you are finally coming to visit me! I'm dying to see you again. It's so long since we last saw each other – it must have been three years ago when we did that summer course. We had such a good time with Luis, Carl and the rest. I wonder what they are all up to now? Have you kept in touch?

When it comes to entertainment, you've chosen a good month to visit. There's lots to do. Make sure you bring your swimming gear. As for getting from the airport to our house, you'd be best off taking a taxi, as you're less likely to get lost! However, if you want something cheaper, there are frequent buses from outside terminal 2 to the town centre. You can check out the bus times on the airport website.

Since you ask about presents, my parents both love chocolate and stuff like that – although you really don't have to bring anything at all. Whatever you do, don't spend loads of money, my parents wouldn't feel comfortable about that.

Love

Maria

2 Read the **how to do it** box and say which of the advice Maria has followed and which she hasn't.

how to do it

Begin by saying something about the email you have received.

Divide what you want to say into different topics in separate paragraphs

Make sure you've included all the information required.

Don't include any unnecessary information.

Check the number of words you have written.

3 Find informal words or phrases in Maria's email that mean a–d.

a   very keen to   c   things of that kind
b   have a look at   d   a large amount of

4 Read the phrases in the language box and say which ones Maria has used.

Expressions for giving advice

Whatever you do, don't …
Make sure you …
Be sure to …
You really must …
You'd be best off (+ *-ing* form)

5 You have received an email from your English-speaking friend, Paula, who is planning to visit you next month. Read her email and the notes you have made. Then write an email reply in 120–150 words.

To:

From: Paula

Subject: Visit

Hi!

I'm really looking forward to seeing you next month. I've just booked my flight. My plane gets in around 4pm, it normally takes about an hour to go through immigration, customs, and so on, so I'll probably get away from the airport around 5pm. What's the best way to get to your house from there?

Give detailed instructions

I'd like to go on a few trips while I'm there. What are the best places to visit? How about coming with me on some of the excursions? Are you going to have much free time next month?

Suggest

I'd better go and look for my passport now. By the way, as you know, I'm starting my art degree next year, so I'd love to visit some museums and galleries while I'm staying with you. Are there any near you?

No, because…

Best wishes

Paula

Give details

Review

1 Complete the sentences with words from the box.

bus driver	visa	ferry	flight attendant
ticket	hand luggage	overhead lockers	scooter

a As well as a passport you'll also need a .... to enter many countries.

b Cars are not allowed on the .... , but you can take a bicycle or ....

c Please try to give the .... the correct money for your ....

d When we got on the plane, the .... told us to store our .... in the ....

2 Choose the correct verb in sentences a–e.

a Our minibus seemed to stop every two minutes to *board/pick up* more passengers.

b Is it a direct service, or do I need to *change/pick up* trains in Boston?

c Ignoring the crowd of journalists, the minister *got into/got onto* his car and drove off.

d It was impossible to leave New York by air that night; the snow meant that all flights had been *cancelled/changed*.

e Passengers must wait in the departure lounge until it is time to *board/get into* the flight.

3 Rewrite sentences a–h to include an appropriate modal verb. Do not change the meaning of the sentences.

a It's essential for you to wear a helmet when you're riding a motorbike.

b From our first floor apartment, we were able to hear noises in the street below.

c It was impossible for us to reach the airport in time.

d Is it OK for me to have a seat by the aisle?

e I advise you not to drink the tap water when you're staying in a hotel.

f It isn't necessary for you to tell me, I already know where you've been!

g Only seven students were able to finish the exam within the time allowed.

h I recommend that she visits the Guggenheim museum while she's in Bilbao.

4 Complete gaps 1–6 in the text with these words and phrases.

as though	as well as	since	in order that
whereas	whether		

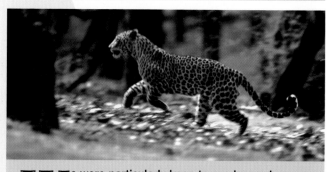

We were particularly keen to see leopards on our safari. Elephants are quite common in this part of Tanzania, (1) .... zebra and antelope, (2) .... leopards are comparatively rare. (3) .... leopards are nocturnal, it was recommended that we go out in the jeep at night. We set off at dusk, and after two hours without any luck, it really felt (4) .... the excursion was going to be a waste of time. Then suddenly, we heard some movement in the bushes. The driver turned off the engine (5) .... the noise wouldn't frighten the animals away, and we waited to find out (6) .... our dreams of seeing a leopard were finally going to come true. And then, with a low growl, a leopardess and her two cubs stepped into the clearing.

5 Complete the second sentence so that it has a similar meaning to the first sentence, using the word given. You must use between two and five words, including the word given.

a The hotel room really wasn't satisfactory.
scratch
The hotel room really .... scratch.

b It was a bumpy flight, and things got even worse after we'd landed.
bad
It was a bumpy flight, and things .... to worse after we'd landed.

c When my parents asked what I wanted for my birthday, I couldn't think of anything.
came
When my parents asked what I wanted for my birthday, ... mind.

d My sister is not bad at tennis, although she doesn't find ball games easy.
easily
My sister is not bad at tennis, although ball games .... to her.

I get the message

Lead in

1 In pairs, discuss which of these forms of communication you use, when you use them and who you communicate with.

a email   e phone

b letter   f video chat

c postcard   g instant messaging

d text message   h chatroom

2 Discuss these questions.

a Are each of a–h in 1 generally more popular with older or younger people? Why?

b What are the advantages and disadvantages of a–h in 1? Think about
- cost
- speed
- convenience
- degree of formality
- the situation (e.g. personal or business)

c Which of a–h in 1 will become more popular in the future, and which less popular, in your opinion? Why?

Reading

Part 3 Multiple matching

1 Imagine you are lost in a remote place and need to signal for help to passing aircraft. Explain how these items might be useful.

2 Read the text opposite about emergency signals to check your ideas from 1. Explain the 'obvious reason' mentioned in the final sentence.

E ARE USED to having a range of different forms of communication at our fingertips 24 hours a day: mobile phones, email, instant messaging … . But imagine a situation in which you are alone in the wilderness, hoping to be rescued, with no way of calling for help. Would
5 you know how to communicate with your potential rescuers? Take a few minutes to learn the codes – they might just save your life!

A SMOKE SIGNALS

During the hours of darkness, fires are the most effective method of signalling. Three fires in a triangle are an international distress signal which pilots and rescue workers everywhere will understand. If you are in a jungle or forest,
10 try to find a clearing, otherwise the fires will not be visible from the air. A burning tree is another way of attracting attention. Always select an isolated tree so that you do not start a forest fire! During the day, fires are also a good way of signalling, provided that they are producing a lot of smoke. The international distress signal is three columns of smoke. Think about what
15 colour the smoke should be in order to stand out against the background. Adding green vegetation to the fire produces white smoke; adding rubber (for example, an old tyre) or clothing soaked in oil produces black smoke.

B MIRROR SIGNALS

On a bright, sunny day, the most effective method of signalling is a mirror.
In fact, pilots have reported seeing mirror flashes up to 160 kilometres
20 away. If you do not have a mirror, any shiny metal surface may work. Aim
the mirror by holding up one finger of your other hand in line with the
aircraft. If you can hear an aircraft but can't see it because of cloud, shine
the mirror in the direction of the noise. Two words of caution, however.
Firstly, do not shine the mirror at the aircraft's cockpit for more than a few
25 seconds, as it might temporarily blind the pilot, which is not what you want
if you are hoping to be spotted. And secondly, if you are in a war zone, do
not flash the mirror rapidly towards the aircraft or the pilot may mistake the
signal for gunfire and avoid the area – or worse, return fire!

C LONG RANGE GROUND-TO-AIR SIGNALS

Once you have been seen by an aircraft, it may be necessary to exchange
30 vital information without the use of a radio. For this reason, internationally
understood signals exist for ground-to-air and air-to-ground communication.
The person on the ground can create the symbols by any means possible
– leaves, branches, gaps in the snow, patterns on the sand – provided they
are large enough to be seen from the air. This usually means at least three
35 metres long and a metre wide. A single line means 'serious injury, doctor
required', while two capital Ls mean 'all is well'. If you have a piece of cloth
big enough, such as a sail or life-raft cover, you can fold it into various
patterns to give information. Folding one corner means 'we need fuel, but
our plane is flyable'. Folding two corners means 'we need warm clothing'.

D BODY SIGNALS AND PILOT'S REPLIES

40 When the aircraft is sufficiently low for the pilot to see you clearly, use
body movements to convey a message. Raising both hands above your
head means 'pick us up' if you keep them still, or 'do not attempt to land
here' if you move your hands to the side in an arc. If the pilot has seen and
understood your signal, he or she will make the aircraft rock from side to
45 side so the wings go up and down. If, however, the message has been seen
but not understood, the aircraft will fly in a clockwise circle overhead. For
obvious reasons, there is no signal which means 'message not seen'!

3 Read the text again carefully.
For questions 1–15, choose from
the sections A–D. The sections
may be chosen more than once.

Which section mentions a
signal which

1 should be made only briefly?
2 is the best one to use at
night?
3 should be in a different
colour according to the
situation?
4 can only be used when an
aircraft is very close?
5 does not require any
equipment or materials?
6 could cause widespread
damage if you chose the
wrong place?
7 could be made with a large
piece of material?
8 can potentially be seen from
very great distances?
9 might use parts of a tree to
make shapes and letters?
10 might involve burning
leaves?
11 can be used to ask for a
message to be repeated?
12 can be used to request
specific items?
13 could be mistaken for an
attack?
14 may work even if the sky is
not clear?
15 involves an aircraft moving
in a particular direction?

4 In pairs, discuss the best way
of making SOS signals in these
different places.

- a rainforest
- a desert
- a mountain range
- a grassy plain

Vocabulary

The verb *get*

> **tip** *get* is a very common verb, especially in spoken English. It has a number of meanings and is used with prepositions and particles to form many phrasal verbs.

1 In three minutes think of as many meanings as you can for the verb *get*. Compare your answers in pairs, then check in a dictionary.

2 Match 1–7 below with the meanings of *get* in sentences a–g.

a I don't get that joke.

b In Iceland it doesn't get dark until about 11 or 12 o'clock in the summer.

c I got a 'B' in my maths exam.

d She always gets hay fever in the summer.

e I can never get my younger daughter to eat any fruit.

f What time did you get here?

g We're getting a new washing machine next week.

1	suffer from (an illness)
2	understand
3	make (someone do something)
4	achieved
5	become
6	arrive
7	buy

Grammar

Passives GR p170–171

1 Read the newspaper article about mobile phone crime, then complete the text beneath it with active verbs instead of passives.

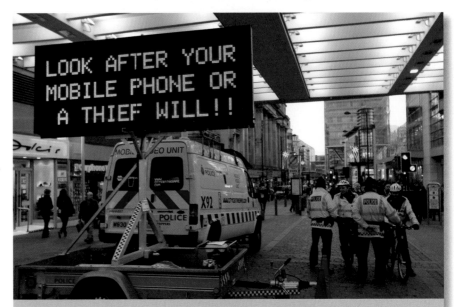

Theft of mobiles on the increase

A **NATIONWIDE CRACKDOWN** on mobile phone crime in Britain is being carried out by police. A police spokesperson said it was believed that 50% of all street crime involved the theft of a mobile phone. Over 73,000 mobile phones are thought to have been stolen in Britain last year – that's 200 a day. Many of them are exported by gangs to Europe, Asia and Africa. Stolen phones can be blocked by the phone networks for use in Britain, but SIM cards can easily be replaced by thieves to make phones usable abroad. The spokesperson added that an international database will be set up by the phone companies to make all stolen handsets useless, whatever their destination.

Police (1) .... a nationwide crackdown on mobile phone crime in Britain. A police spokesperson said they (2) .... that 50% of all street crime involved the theft of a mobile phone. Police (3) .... that over 73,000 mobile phones were stolen in Britain last year – that's 200 a day. Gangs (4) .... many of them to Europe, Asia and Africa. The phone networks (5) .... stolen phones for use in Britain, but the thieves can easily (6) .... SIM cards to make phones usable abroad. The spokesperson added that the phone companies (7) .... an international database to make all stolen handsets useless, whatever their destination.

2 Complete these extracts from radio reports using the correct verbs in the passive form.

hold	catch	arrest	discover

'A man **1**_____ by police last night after he **2**_____ shoplifting in a local store. Several thousand pounds' worth of jewellery **3**_____ in his pockets. He **4**_____ in police custody until he appears in court tomorrow.'

convict	fine	find	stop

'Carl Hancock, a retired doctor, **5**_____ £500 after **6**_____ of drunken driving. His car **7**_____ by police officers on the motorway and he **8**_____ to have 150 milligrammes of alcohol in his blood, almost twice the legal limit.'

3 Find examples of *subject + modal verb + passive infinitive* in the article in 1. Then complete a–f using the passive infinitive and the words in brackets.

a This film _____ (can/see) at cinemas all over the country.

b In Japan, shoes _____ (must not/wear) in the house.

c The new football stadium _____ (should/complete) before 2012.

d The 9/11 terrorists _____ (should never/be allowed) onto the planes.

e John F Kennedy _____ (might not/kill) by Lee Harvey Oswald.

f Look at the postmark. This letter _____ (must/post) in London.

4 Find examples of these structures in the article in 1.

a *It* + passive + *that* clause

b subject + passive + infinitive

5 Rewrite sentences a–f in the passive, as in the example.

Example In the past people thought that swimming in the sea was bad for you.

In the past it was thought that swimming in the sea was bad for you.

In the past swimming in the sea was thought to be bad for you.

a Someone reported that a coach collided with a lorry on the motorway last night.

b They thought the politician was telling the truth.

c People believe the police have arrested the wrong man.

d They expect that Mary will pass all her exams.

e People consider that he is one of the finest writers alive.

f They believe that the woman was driving too fast when she crashed into the tree.

6 Read sentences 1 and 2 below and answer these questions.

a How many objects does *owe* have in sentence 1? Which is the direct object and which is the indirect object?

b In sentence 2, which object becomes the subject of the passive verb: the direct object, or the indirect object?

1 My brother owes me £50.

2 I'm owed £50 by my brother.

7 Make sentences a–e passive as in the example. Include the agent, thinking carefully about its best position in the sentence.

Example My boss offered me a promotion at work.

I was offered a promotion at work by my boss.

a Mr Fielding teaches us English.

b The online store will send me a receipt in the post.

c The kidnappers have given him two days to pay the ransom.

d My wife read the children a bedtime story.

e Her secretary brought her two letters to sign.

Listening

Part 3 Multiple matching

1 �))) You will hear five people talking about misunderstandings. Match the speakers with misunderstandings A–F. There is one extra letter.

Speaker 1 ....

Speaker 2 ....

Speaker 3 ....

Speaker 4 ....

Speaker 5 ....

A went to the wrong meeting place

B gave someone the wrong information

C misheard directions to a place

D misunderstood some instructions

E misunderstood an invitation

F went to a meeting they weren't invited to

2 �))) Complete sentences a–f from the recording with the correct phrasal verb, then listen again and check your answers.

a So we .... off and I didn't bother to check where we were going on the map.

b We got hopelessly lost because I'd .... down the wrong road.

c What <u>was</u> a problem was that Becky didn't .... up.

d It .... out that they needed to discuss what projects they were going to give me!

e He said they usually .... together with a set of old friends from university, but why didn't we .... round for a drink.

f There was a big sales conference .... up.

3 In pairs, tell each other about a misunderstanding that you have been involved in. Use the phrases below to help you.

- I was under the impression that ...
- I thought that ... but in fact ...
- Naturally I assumed that ...
- It turned out that ...
- It was so embarrassing.
- I was horrified.
- I felt awful.
- I felt such a fool.
- We had a good laugh about it.

Speaking

Part 3 and 4

1 What would be the advantages of doing a language course in an English-speaking country, rather than in your own country? Would there be any disadvantages?

2 Look at the adverts for a language school that wants to attract 14–16-year-olds to its summer courses. Discuss these questions.

a How successful would the advertisements be?

b Which two would attract more students?

3 �))) Listen to two students doing a Part 4 task. Tick the questions the examiner asks and say which candidate gives better answers.

a Would you like to take a course at The Regal Language School?

b What are the advantages and disadvantages of studying English abroad?

c What are the advantages and disadvantages of having an English teacher who cannot speak your own language?

d Why do you think it's important to study foreign languages?

4 Read the **how to do it** box. Then work in groups of three and follow these instructions.

STUDENT A: You are the examiner. Ask some of the questions in 3. Use the phrases in the **tip** box to involve both Students B and C in the discussion. Keep the discussion going for about three minutes.

STUDENTS B and C: You are the candidates. Answer the questions. Give reasons for your opinions.

how to do it

Listen to the examiner's questions.

Ask for repetition if necessary.

Give a full, confident answer.

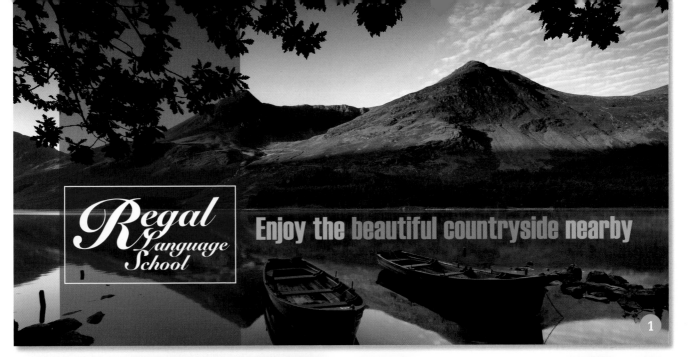

Regal Language School

Enjoy the beautiful countryside nearby

1

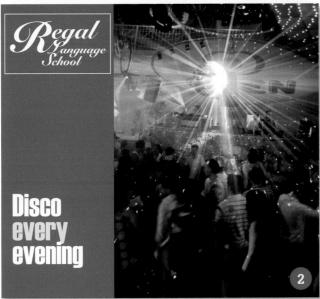

Regal Language School

Disco every evening

2

3

Regal Language School

Make friends from other countries

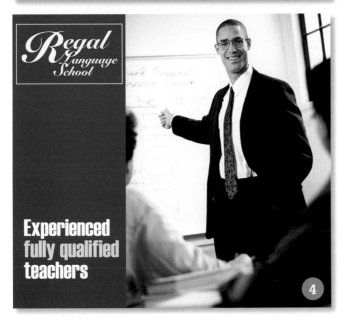

Regal Language School

4

Experienced fully qualified teachers

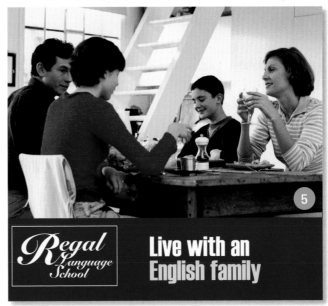

5

Regal Language School

Live with an English family

Use of English

Part 1 Multiple-choice cloze

1 Rewrite sentences a–g replacing the underlined words with the correct form of these phrasal verbs. Use your dictionary if necessary.

> get at   get down   get in   get on   get out of
> get through   get up to

a How did you <u>avoid</u> going to that dreadful party?

b What page have you <u>reached</u> in the book you're reading?

c We've <u>used</u> six litres of milk since your parents arrived.

d Give me a break, will you? You're always <u>criticising</u> me.

e What really <u>depresses</u> me about winter is the long cold evenings.

f What time does your flight <u>arrive</u>?

g 'Grandad's getting very forgetful.' 'Well, he's <u>growing older</u>, isn't he?'

2 Quickly read the text opposite, ignoring the gaps. Has anything similar to the incidents described ever happened to you or someone you know?

EMAILS THEY WISH THEY'D NEVER SENT

Email is a wonderful .... (0) of communication. It's easy, it's fast – but sometimes just one little click of the 'send' button can spell disaster.

How many times have emails been sent to the .... (1) person, or to several people .... (2) just one person? Dave Gethings got .... (3) trouble when he replied to a birthday invitation. He emailed back a joking, but extremely rude reply, not only to his friend, but also to his manager, the secretaries, directors – to .... (4) in the company, in fact.

There are other cases of people forwarding emails .... (5) purpose. Lawyer Richard Phillips emailed his secretary .... (6) her that she had spilt tomato ketchup on his trousers at lunch and asking her to pay the dry-cleaning bill for the .... (7) of £4. This email, which was passed around many other law firms, was answered with a stinging reply by his secretary, which also went round the legal world and even .... (8) it into the national news! With the resulting publicity, Mr Phillips was so embarrassed at .... (9) people considered to be his meanness that he left his job.

Joseph Dobbie said that he wasn't embarrassed when his email was .... (10) around the world, but he did have to change his telephone numbers. He had sent a romantic email to a woman called Kate, who he had met at a party. She had sent it to her sister, who forwarded it to friends, who then forwarded it to more friends. In the end he was getting .... (11) from people as .... (12) away as Australia and the US!

So, before we send our next email, perhaps we should stop and think …

3 Read the **how to do it** box. Then read the text again carefully and for 1–12 decide which answer (A, B, C or D) best fits each gap.

how to do it

Read the text quickly, ignoring the gaps, to get the general meaning.

Read the text carefully, and for each gap, think of a possible answer before looking at the option.

Try each option in the gap before deciding.

0	A	way	7	A	sum
	B	means		B	amount
	C	model		C	money
	D	result		D	quantity
1	A	mistaken	8	A	did
	B	false		B	got
	C	bad		C	made
	D	wrong		D	took
2	A	rather	9	A	what
	B	other than		B	that
	C	in place of		C	why
	D	instead of		D	which
3	A	to	10	A	recycled
	B	at		B	circled
	C	into		C	circulated
	D	up to		D	cycled
4	A	anyone	11	A	calls
	B	everyone		B	rings
	C	someone		C	talks
	D	all		D	phones
5	A	for	12	A	long
	B	on		B	distant
	C	to		C	remote
	D	in		D	far
6	A	writing			
	B	saying			
	C	telling			
	D	replying			

(In item 0, B "means" is circled.)

Vocabulary

Phrasal verbs

1 Decide which verbs are more appropriate in these sentences – the phrasal verbs or the more formal equivalents.

a Please note that candidates may not *leave out/omit* more than two questions.

b Did you read about that guy who stole loads of library books? They should *lock him up/imprison him* when they get him.

c Come on mum. *Speed up/Accelerate* a bit or we'll never get there.

d Further to our recent telephone conversation, I am *sending back/returning* the faulty camera in question and *asking for/requesting* a full refund.

e Hang on, I need to *work out/calculate* how much money this is going to cost me!

f Guests are kindly requested to *get out of/vacate* their rooms by 11 a.m. on the day of departure.

2 Read sentences 1–4 below, then do the following.

a Match the phrasal verbs in brackets with a verb it can replace in the sentence.

b Rewrite each sentence using the phrasal verbs.

1 I'd love to discover why Jack rejected the offer of a free holiday with me, so try to raise the topic when you speak to him! (*bring up, find out, turn down*)

2 We departed early in the morning, but we encountered heavy traffic on the motorway, which really delayed us. (*hold up, run into, set off*)

3 Wait a minute. Are you saying that you submitted the application form without completing your name and address? (*fill in, hang on, send in*)

4 My brother didn't confess to breaking the window – instead he invented some story about two men throwing a brick then escaping on a motorbike. (*own up, make off, make up*)

Writing

Part 1 An informal email

1 Is there anyone you have lost touch with who you'd like to meet up with again? How could you get in touch with them?

2 Read the email from Patricia and number the paragraphs of Sophie's reply below in the correct order.

New Message

To: **Sophie**

From: **Patricia**

Subject: **Friends Forever**

Dear Sophie,

Saw your name on the *Friends Forever* website. Do you remember me – Pat Nichols from college? *Yes! I remember...*

What have you been up to since we last saw each other?

I'll be in London next month from the 20th to 25th. Any chance of meeting up? If so, let me know when and where.

Best wishes

Patricia Nichols

Tell her.

Ask for news of her.

Yes. Suggest.

New Message

To: **Patricia**

From: **Sophie**

Subject: **RE: Friends Forever**

Dear Pat,

☐ So much has happened since we last met – I hardly know where to start. After leaving school I spent a couple of years abroad, doing a bit of voluntary work and teaching English in Peru. That's where I met my husband, Fernando. Anyway, we came back about two years ago. Fernando teaches Spanish at a local college.

☐ Can't wait to see you again! Email again soon with your news and bring me up to date.

☐ Thanks so much for your email. Yes, I do remember you! We used to be really good mates, didn't we, when we were at school?

☐ It would be really great to see you again! I can easily get down to London while you're there. The 23rd would be best for me. Why don't we meet up for dinner?

Love

Sophie

3 Find examples in Sophie's email of these features of informal language.

  a phrasal verbs
  b contractions
  c informal expressions
  d short sentences
  e frequent use of exclamation marks
  f omission of the subject pronoun

4 Rewrite the paragraph below, using the features mentioned in 3. You may need to replace a word, add something, or delete something.

> I received your email about two days ago. I am glad that you are enjoying yourself, but I was sorry to hear that they rejected your application to go to university. What a shame. When will you discover if you can study at another university instead? Anyway, please, please reply soon and I hope to see you again before too long.

5 Add phrases a–f to the language boxes, then check your answers in Sophie's email.

  a Keep in touch
  b Thanks so much for your …
  c Love/Lots of love
  d It was a nice surprise to get your …
  e Take care
  f Email again soon.

●●● Reacting to the input

Great to hear from you.

●●● Finishing an email

Look forward to seeing you soon.

●●● Signing off

Best wishes

6 You have just received this email from an old friend that you haven't seen for a while. Write a reply (120–150 words) following the paragraph plan below.

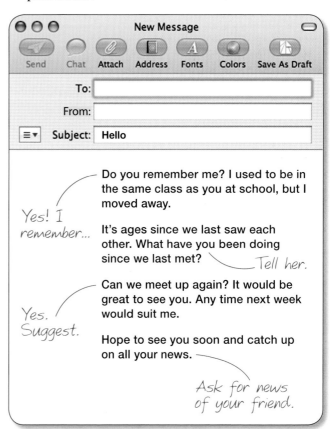

> Paragraph 1 say you remember him/her, and where and when
>
> Paragraph 2 say what you have been doing since you last saw each other
>
> Paragraph 3 invite your friend to your house for a meal
>
> Paragraph 4 ask for his/her news

Review

1 Rewrite sentences a–g using another verb to replace *get*.

  a I couldn't get the shop to give me a refund.

  b Tom's very lucky – he never gets coughs or colds.

  c I really don't get the point of what you're saying.

  d The ship got smaller and smaller before disappearing over the horizon.

  e What time did you get home last night?

  f Sam got the highest possible score in his music exam.

  g When did you get that digital camera?

2 Complete the phrasal verbs with *get* in sentences a–g.

  a His father insisted that Robert did his homework before dinner. He couldn't get .... it.

  b It really gets me .... when you don't do your share of the housework.

  c My dad's getting .... He's nearly seventy.

  d In the last lesson we got .... page 34 of the Student's Book.

  e We got .... six packets of crisps while we were watching the film.

  f Stop getting .... your brother. It isn't fair to criticise him like that all the time.

  g The train got .... ten minutes late so I missed my connection.

3 Match phrasal verbs a–f with their more formal equivalents 1–6.

  a work out   1 invent
  b set off   2 confess
  c turn down   3 accelerate
  d make up   4 reject
  e own up   5 calculate
  f speed up   6 depart

4 Complete the sentences with an appropriate verb from 3.

  a I can't .... the answers to any of these maths questions!

  b We didn't want to go to the cinema, so we .... an excuse.

  c In order to escape the earth's gravity, a rocket needs to .... to approximately 11 kilometres per second.

  d We .... really early to avoid the rush-hour traffic.

  e Jason .... my invitation to our house-warming party.

  f Come on! ....! Who put salt in my tea?

5 Complete each gap 1–8 in this email with an appropriate word.

> ⬤⬤⬤   New Message   ⬭
>
> To: _____
>
> From: _____
>
> ≡▾ Subject: Hello
>
> Hi Sue,
>
> Thanks so [1] .... for your email. Yes, I [2] .... remember you! We [3] .... to be next-door neighbours, didn't we? A lot has happened [4] .... we last met, 10 years ago.
>
> Why don't we meet [5] .... somewhere and have lunch? One day next week [6] .... be best for me.
>
> I [7] .... wait to see you again. Write again soon with more news and bring me [8] .... to date.
>
> Love
>
> Tania

A matter of taste

Lead in

1 ◉ Listen to five people describing how to make a dish from their country. Match the speakers with the photos and say which countries you think the dishes are from.

Speaker	Photo
1	....
2	....
3	....
4	....
5	....

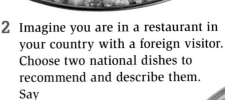

A

2 Imagine you are in a restaurant in your country with a foreign visitor. Choose two national dishes to recommend and describe them. Say

- if it's a savoury dish or a sweet dish
- when you eat it
- what the main ingredients are and how it's cooked.

B

3 In pairs, discuss the following.

a Is it very important to you what you eat? What foods do you particularly enjoy eating?

b What foods do you dislike? What is it about them you don't like? Think about taste, smell, texture and appearance.

c Do you enjoy cooking? Why/ Why not?

C

D

E

Reading

Part 2 Gapped text

1 What kind of restaurants do you prefer eating in? Why?

2 Read the text opposite quickly, ignoring the gaps, to find out what is unusual about the two restaurants described. Then explain what is happening in the photo at the bottom right of the page.

3 Read the text again carefully and the **how to do it** box, then match sentences A–H with gaps 1–7. There is one extra sentence.

  A He believes that your sense of taste is intensified if you are not distracted by what you can see.

  B He, after all, was the one who brought us snail porridge and bacon ice-cream.

  C They want their guests to concentrate solely on the food that is in front of them.

  D The first does so by excluding other sensory input altogether.

  E On the other hand, it must be a very strange experience for diners.

  F The seafood dish looks like a picture of the seashore.

  G Then you are led to your table in the pitch-black dining room by a blind waiter.

  H Some critics claim that diners will lose out on the social side of dining.

 how to do it

Read the text quickly to get the general idea.

Look for links with grammar and vocabulary before and after each gap and in the sentences.

Fill the easiest gaps first.

Try the extra sentence in each gap again.

Read the text again, checking your answers.

4 Discuss the question in the final sentence of the text, giving reasons.

The Great Taste Sensation

WHY do we eat out in restaurants? Eating out is usually about more than just the taste of the food. But for two restaurant owners in the south of England, this lack of focus is unacceptable. **1** Interestingly, they set about achieving this in completely different ways.

Would you be happy to eat something if you couldn't see it? Edouard de Broglie, the restaurateur behind the new London restaurant 'Dans le Noir', hopes so. **2** 'Dans le Noir' is French for 'in the dark' and it is a blacked-out restaurant, where blind waiters and waitresses serve your food. **3** Others accept that the darkness brings an added sense of intimacy. De Broglie, who set up the original, and very successful, 'Dans le Noir' restaurant in Paris, said that his interest was in the sensory not the social aspects of dining. 'The preconception of what food tastes like because of how it looks is gone,' he said. 'All your other senses are abruptly awoken and you taste the food like you have never tasted it before.'

This is how the restaurant works. When you arrive you can choose from the menu in the brightly lit reception area. **4** You will have to feel for your cutlery, try to find the food on your plate, and try not to spill your wine! Fortunately, all glasses are made from unbreakable glass. According to Dr Charles Spence, an Oxford University lecturer in experimental psychology, everybody should try it. He said, 'We are visually dominant creatures driven by our eyes and anything you can do to change that is a worthwhile venture.'

Heston Blumenthal, chef and owner of the famous restaurant 'The Fat Duck' near London, has long been renowned for his adventurous menus and experimental cooking. **5** But even his most extraordinary dishes will seem dull and ordinary compared with his latest creation – seafood served with an iPod.

No, diners will not be expected to eat the music player, but instead to listen to the noise of crashing waves as they eat. The dish, entitled 'Sound Of The Sea', will be part of the tasting menu at the three-Michelin-starred restaurant. **6** It is presented on a glass-topped wooden box containing sand and seashells, and consists of what looks like sand but is in fact a mixture of fried breadcrumbs, fried baby eels and oil, topped with different kinds of seafood, oysters and three kinds of edible seaweed, all arranged beautifully. The final touch – resulting from Blumenthal's experiments exploring the relationship between sound and the experience of eating – will be the iPod, so that diners can listen to the sound of the sea while they eat.

Blumenthal strongly believes that the sound of the waves intensifies the taste experience of eating seafood. 'I did a series of tests with Dr Charles Spence at Oxford University three years ago,' he said, 'which revealed that sound can really enhance the sense of taste. We ate an oyster while listening to the sea and it tasted stronger and saltier, for example.'

Both of these restaurants seek to intensify the sensation of taste while you are eating. **7** The second does so by adding to it. So which eating experience would appeal more to *your* senses?

Vocabulary

Food

1 Say whether these adjectives are positive, negative or neutral, depending on the context.

> bitter   chewy   crunchy   fatty   greasy   mild
> plain   rich   salty   spicy   stodgy   sweet
> tasteless   tasty   tender

2 Decide which adjectives from 1 you would use to describe these foods and drinks.

> curry   olives   ice-cream   fried chicken
> steak   boiled rice   coffee

3 Match the methods of cooking with pictures 1–7. Give an example of one kind of food that is often prepared in each way.

> fried   boiled   roast   grilled   barbecued
> baked   stewed

Grammar

Speculating about the present and past GR p170–171

1 Read sentences 1–6 and do the following.

a Underline the modal verb in each of 1–6.

b Match the meanings of the modal verbs with these phrases.
- I'm sure it's true that …
- It's possibly true that …
- I'm sure it isn't true that …

c Say which refer to the present, and which to the past.

1 That fish can't be cooked yet. It's only been under the grill for two minutes.

2 This meat is a bit dry and chewy. The chef must have overcooked it.

3 There were three tins of olives in the cupboard. We can't have eaten them all, can we?

4 Don't take the chicken out of the freezer yet. We might be eating out tonight if I can book a table.

5 You haven't eaten a thing since yesterday lunchtime. You must be starving.

6 I feel really ill. I think I might have eaten something that disagreed with me.

2 Rewrite sentences a–e using *must, might or can't*, as in the example.

Example   I'm sure you are joking.

    You must be joking.

a   It's possible that he'll give you a ring this evening.

b   I'm sure Patricia isn't wearing her scarf. I saw it hanging on the hook on the back door.

c   I'm certain that James has got my mobile. I let him use it to call his sister this morning.

d   I'm sure that isn't Jim over there. His hair isn't as long as that.

e   I can possibly give you a hand with the cooking if I get home in good time.

3 Think of appropriate replies to these sentences using *must, might* or *can't*.

a   I feel hot and I've got a headache.

b   I've just seen a ghost.

c   I'm eating at a really expensive restaurant this evening.

d   My best friend has just been given the sack.

e   I had an argument with my best friend last night.

f   I've had enough. I'm going to live on a desert island.

4 Complete the sentences with the verbs in the box in the correct form. Use *must have, might have,* and *can't have.*

~~be~~	eat	invent	leave	spend
spill	stir	write down		

Example   Even the cat didn't eat the fish. It <u>must have been</u> bad.

a   His breath smells awful. He .... a lot of garlic last night.

b   This sauce has gone all lumpy. I .... it properly.

c   Beer .... in Iran about 7,000 years ago, but nobody's quite sure.

d   What a fantastic spread. You .... ages preparing all this food.

e   'Where are my keys?' 'You .... them in the restaurant, or possibly in the car.'

f   I didn't order tomato soup. The waiter .... the order correctly.

g   'There's a horrible stain on my new shirt. I .... some food on it.'

5 Look at the photos. Speculate about them using *must (have), might (have) and can't (have)*, as in the example.

Example   He must be hungry.

Listening

Part 3 Multiple matching

1 In pairs, tell each other about the last time you ate out. Say

- who you went with and why
- what you ate
- what the restaurant and food were like
- whether you'd recommend the restaurant to a friend

how to do it

Before you listen, read options A–F carefully.

As you listen, answer as many of the questions as you can.

When you listen again, concentrate on the answers you are least certain of.

2 You will hear five people talking about a problem they had when eating out. Read the **How to do it** box, then match the speakers with the problems A–F. There is one extra letter.

Speaker 1 ....

Speaker 2 ....

Speaker 3 ....

Speaker 4 ....

Speaker 5 ....

A ate in a different restaurant from the one they'd booked

B had to wait a while for a table

C ended up cooking at home

D booked a table but couldn't find the restaurant

E ended up eating a takeaway

F had to wait a while for the food

3 Tell a partner about any bad experiences you've had when eating out. Think about

- booking a table
- finding a restaurant
- arrangements to meet
- food
- service

Speaking

Parts 3 and 4

1 Look at the pictures of different restaurants and match this description to one of them.

Example   It looks very traditional and formal. I expect the food is dear, possibly over-priced. I expect it's quite quiet, too.

2 In pairs take it in turns to describe one of the restaurants using the words below to help you. Your partner should guess which one you are describing.

boring	cramped	dear	exciting	formal
friendly	value for money		informal	lively
noisy	overpriced	quiet	romantic	
traditional	trendy			

3 Listen to two people discussing where to eat. Do they manage to come to an agreement?

4 Listen again and number sentences a–h in the order you hear them.

a Can't we go somewhere more upmarket? ....

b *Gianni's* is OK but it's a bit too quiet. ....

c I don't fancy an Indian. ....

d I expect the food's a bit basic. ....

e I'd prefer somewhere quieter. ....

f I'm not that keen on Chinese food. ....

g It looks very noisy. ....

h The service is terrible. ....

5 In pairs, imagine that you are planning a meal out with friends to celebrate the end of your exams. Discuss how suitable each of the restaurants shown might be and decide which one to go to.

6 Work in groups of three and do the following.

- Student 1: ask Students 2 and 3 question a) below. Students 2 and 3 answer, giving reasons.

- Student 2: ask Students 1 and 3 question b), etc.

a In your country, what are the most popular types of foreign food? Which do you prefer? Why?

b Are takeaways popular in your country? Why? What sort in particular?

c Have you ever worked in a restaurant? If so, what was it like? If not, would you like to? Why?/Why not?

Use of English

Part 3 Word formation

●●● Adjective suffixes

We can add suffixes to nouns or verbs to make them into adjectives.
Sometimes the spelling changes.

-y	-ous
chew > chewy	mystery > mysterious
-al	**-ful**
music > musical	hope > hopeful
-able	**-less**
rely > reliable	use > useless

We can often use different suffixes with the same word to create
adjectives with different meanings:

taste: *tasty* – delicious *tasteful* – attractive *tasteless* – without taste; inappropriate

1 Read the information about adjective suffixes. Which suffix forms a negative adjective?

2 Work in pairs. In two minutes, think of as many adjectives as possible with the endings
in the box.

3 Complete sentences a–g with an appropriate adjective formed from the word in brackets.

Example   Tom's cousin is a .... singer. (fame)

Tom's cousin is a famous singer.

a   She may seem a bit cold and distant at times, but Cathy is a very kind and
.... woman. (thought)
b   It was .... of Harry not to invite his best friend to his new girlfriend's party. (thought)
c   I first visited Madrid on .... a day in September. (rain)
d   They've opened a night shelter for .... people in our area. (home)
e   He's so .... about tennis that he plays it three times a week. (fanatic)
f   This coffee isn't great but it's .... if you're desperate! (drink)
g   Many medicines are .... if you take more than the recommended dose. (harm)

4 Read the text opposite, then complete each gap with a word formed from 1–10.

0	say	6	pleasure
1	harm	7	tired
2	sugar	8	laugh
3	moderate	9	health
4	meet	10	absolute
5	open		

5 Find four gaps in the text in 4 where you have to make an adjective from a noun.

6 Do you agree with the advice given in the text?

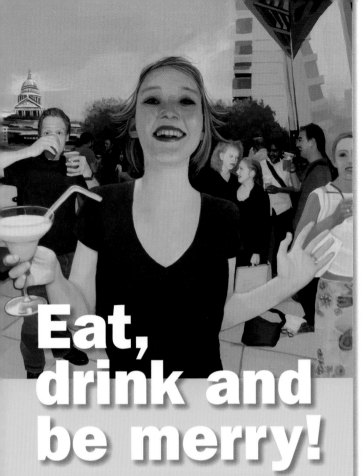

Eat, drink and be merry!

.... **so the (0) saying goes.** But until recently, doctors have been telling us to do exactly the opposite, warning us that overeating is (1) .... Now it seems, rich, fatty foods or sweet, (2) .... ones, can be perfectly good for us in (3) .... , but only under certain circumstances.

Recently, at a three-day (4) .... in Venice, a group of doctors, psychologists, and chemists met to discuss the importance of pleasure on our health. They celebrated the (5) .... of the conference by feasting on venison and truffles.

The point that they were there to discuss is that things that are (6) .... and make us feel good have a positive effect on our health and wellbeing. Guilt, stress, and (7) .... lead to illness. Pleasure, (8) .... and love, including eating things that are generally considered bad for you, keep our immune systems strong and therefore improve our health.

However, it is important to realise that we mustn't eat too much (9) .... food, and when we do, we must really enjoy it. There's (10) .... no point in eating a bar of chocolate and then feeling guilty about it, because that creates a double negative – it is unhealthy and has given you no enjoyment! Remember, eat, drink and be MERRY!

Vocabulary

●●● **Word** pairs

There are many word pairs that are joined by a conjunction. The order of the words is fixed.

bread and butter	wait and see

Sometimes the words in the pair are near synonyms.

fun and games	law and order

Sometimes the words in the pair are opposites.

take it or leave it	give and take

1 Read the information about word pairs. Make sure you understand the meaning of the examples, then match a–e with 1–5.

a	sick	1	sound
b	pick	2	tired
c	safe	3	choose
d	peace	4	pieces
e	bits	5	quiet

2 Say whether the word pairs in 1 are
- verb + verb
- noun + noun
- adjective + adjective

3 Complete word pairs a–e with opposites, then check your answers in a dictionary.

a more or ....
b back to ....
c sooner or ....
d now and ....
e ups and ....

4 Rewrite sentences a–g replacing the underlined phrases with pairs of words from 1 and 2.

a I've had enough of your complaining! Give it a rest, will you?
b Eventually Steve will realise his mistake.
c John spent his summer holiday travelling up the Amazon, but he's arrived home healthy and unharmed.
d As a child, I had to eat what I was given. I wasn't allowed to have only what I liked.
e The UK is approximately 1,200 kilometres long from north to south.
f We hardly ever eat out but occasionally we get a take-away.
g 'Have you moved all that rubbish out of the spare room yet?' 'Nearly. There are just a few small things left.'

Writing

Part 2 A report

1 What facilities are or were available in your school?

2 Read the task and the report, ignoring the underlining. Decide whether the report
   a supports the idea
   b opposes the idea
   c recommends a different course of action.

> The director of your language school has put forward an idea to remove the only food and drinks machine. You have been asked to find out the views of your fellow students and write a report with your recommendation.

REPORT ON IDEA TO REMOVE FOOD AND DRINKS MACHINE

Introduction
The <u>aim</u> of this report is to <u>consider</u> the <u>pros and cons</u> of removing the food and drinks machine from the student common room, and to make a recommendation to the director of the school.

Advantages
There are some strong arguments <u>in favour of</u> removing the machine. It is felt that it:
- is old, ugly and noisy.
- takes up valuable space.
- sells only unhealthy foods, such as crisps, sweets and fizzy drinks.

Disadvantages
Removing the machine would also have <u>drawbacks</u>.
- A lot of students use it and would be unhappy if it were removed.
- The machine saves people valuable time as they do not have to go out and buy snacks at the local shops.

Conclusion
Although there are <u>convincing</u> arguments for removing the machine, I believe <u>on balance</u> that the disadvantages of doing so outweigh the advantages. However, I recommend that it is replaced with a smaller, more modern model that has a wider range of snacks, including some healthy ones.

tip Use headings and numbered or bullet points.
Try to use synonyms rather than repeat words.

3 Under which heading does the writer do the following?

a   list the arguments against the idea
b   make a recommendation
c   state the aim of the report
d   list the arguments for the idea

4 Read the **tip** box, then match the words and phrases below with the synonyms underlined in the report.

a   advantages and disadvantages
b   strong
c   examine
d   disadvantages
e   for
f   purpose
g   after considering all the information

5 Read the task below, then divide sentences a–h into two groups: arguments for and arguments against the idea. Add any other arguments you can think of.

> **The director of the school suggests closing the canteen and using the space for a student recreation room, with a TV and pool table. You have been asked to write a report on the advantages and disadvantages of this idea.**

a   The canteen is underused.
b   The canteen food isn't very good.
c   The canteen food is cheap.
d   The canteen is very popular.
e   There's an excellent café opposite the school.
f   Students need a place to relax between and after lessons.
g   There's a TV in the café opposite the school.
h   Pool is popular among boys but not among girls.

6 Write a report of between 120 and 180 words. Divide your report into four sections, using the same headings as in the model report in 2. Use some of the arguments in 5.

Review

1 Choose the correct adjectives to complete a–e.

a This pork isn't very *stodgy/tender*. I should have cooked it for longer.

b I like nice green *crunchy/chewy* apples.

c These grapes are incredibly *rich/bitter*.

d 'How's your meal?' 'The bacon's OK but the fried eggs are rather *greasy/fatty*.'

e Crisps usually have a *mild/salty* taste.

2 Complete a–f using an adjective formed from the words in the box.

finance	forget	fury	penny	suit	wonder

a We saw a _____ play at the theatre last night.

b My dad was _____ when I stayed out all night.

c Grandad is getting more and more _____ as he gets older.

d He was _____ when he came to this country, but now he's a millionaire.

e The hotel doesn't have any rooms that are _____ for families.

f My brother works for a bank in the _____ district of Frankfurt.

3 Complete a–e with word pairs from the box using *and* or *or*.

give	later	less	more	safe	see
sooner	sound	take	wait		

a We were nearly involved in an accident on the motorway but we arrived home _____ .

b 'What's for pudding, mum?' '_____ . You haven't finished your first course yet.'

c The journey may take a long time, but we'll get there _____ .

d 'Is this the kind of thing you had in mind?' 'Yes, _____ .'

e If little Jimmy doesn't learn to _____ he won't make friends very easily.

4 For a–e complete the second sentence so that it has a similar meaning to the first sentence using the word given. Use between two and five words, including the word given. Do not change the word given.

a I'm sure you'll find your keys in the end.
   turn
   Your keys _____ later.

b It was very careless of you to spill coffee on the new rug.
   careful
   If you _____ you wouldn't have spilt coffee on the new rug.

c I've had enough of reality shows on TV.
   tired
   I'm sick _____ reality shows on TV.

d Linda thinks it's a good idea to install a new coffee machine.
   favour
   Linda is _____ a new coffee machine.

e This curry isn't spicy enough.
   mild
   This curry _____ .

5 Complete these lines from reports with the following words and phrases.

cons	convincing	drawback	examine
on balance	pros	purpose	

The .... of this report is to .... the .... and .... of the proposal to buy more computers for the school.

The most .... argument is that the computers are too slow for broadband Internet.

The only .... seems to be that there would be less money to spend on books in the coming year.

.... I think that the proposal is worth recommending.

Going to extremes

Lead in

1 Look at the photos. What do you think these people's obsessions or particular habits might be?

2)) **Listen and match the speakers with sentences a–e.**

a I'm a terrible time-keeper.
b I can never throw things away.
c I'm a shopaholic.
d I'm really untidy.
e I'm obsessively well organised.

Speaker	Sentence
1	....
2	....
3	....
4	....
5	....

3 Discuss these questions.

a Are the characteristics in 2 generally good or bad?
b Do you have any particular habits (good or bad)?
c How easy is it to learn new habits or stop bad ones?

Reading

Part 1 Multiple choice

1 Discuss whether you agree or disagree with the statement below. Give examples to support your opinion.

> You can't experience **real** excitement without taking risks.

2 The article opposite is about people who take risks. Read the text quickly and find the names of the two people in the photos.

3 Find these adjectives in the text and explain their meanings in the context in your own words.

   a countless (l. 12)
   b tiny (l. 20)
   c inhospitable (l. 35)
   d furious (l. 40)
   e even (l. 46)
   f major (l. 50)
   g single-minded (l. 63)
   h addictive (l. 66)

4 Read the text again carefully and for questions 1–8, choose the best answer (A, B, C or D).

  1 According to the text, most people would prefer to have
     A a comfortable life without risk.
     B occasional chances to test their endurance.
     C some experience of danger.
     D fewer unpleasant tasks in their lives.

  2 Kanchana Ketkeaw did not suffer serious injury from the scorpions because
     A they did not sting her.
     B scorpion stings are not very dangerous.
     C she did not allow the scorpions to touch her body.
     D her body has become used to the poison.

  3 The writer of the text believes that Kanchana Ketkeaw
     A is a bit mad.
     B was asked to perform her feat by her country.
     C did not perform her feat only for her country.
     D does not know why she performed her feat.

  4 When did Lynne Cox first discover that she enjoyed swimming in difficult conditions?
     A in her forties
     B when she was nine
     C between the ages of nine and fourteen
     D at the age of fourteen

  5 Why is Lynne Cox particularly well suited to what she does?
     A Her style of swimming is similar to a seal's.
     B She likes swimming in outdoor pools.
     C She's rather fat.
     D Unusually, the fat below her skin has a regular thickness.

  6 In both of the expeditions mentioned, Sir Ranulph Fiennes
     A suffered physical injury.
     B endured very severe weather conditions.
     C discovered ancient ruins.
     D spent several years away from home.

  7 Sir Ranulph Fiennes uses the memory of his father
     A to give him strength at difficult moments.
     B to remind him of the limits of human endurance.
     C to remind him that death is always a risk.
     D to help him make difficult decisions.

  8 Adventurers find that they cannot stop taking risks because
     A they have become famous for risk-taking.
     B their lives are less stable than other people's.
     C they love the feeling it produces.
     D they believe they can achieve the impossible.

5 Which of the three people in the article do you admire, if any? Why?

AGAINST ALL ODDS

Why do some people feel compelled to do the craziest things, while most of us are happy to sit on the sofa and watch their exploits on TV? Robin Styles ponders this question.

5 **Generally,** we love to watch someone's bravery and drama – a single person against the wilds of nature, testing their endurance beyond belief. And our pleasure is greater because we live in a comfortable world of central heating, gadgets and package holidays. We lead increasingly risk-
10 free lives, where the greatest test of endurance is getting to work through the rush hour. And most of us would prefer it to remain that way. However, there are countless ways to test the limits of your endurance, should you wish to do so, by attempting something unpleasant,
15 uncomfortable or just plain dangerous.

Thirty-year-old performance artist, Kanchana Ketkeaw, who spent 32 days and nights in a scorpion-filled room, said that she completed her amazing feat of endurance for her country, Thailand. The new world record holder
20 shared a tiny room for over a month with 3,400 deadly little friends, and was stung at least nine times! Fortunately she has worked with scorpions
25 for several years now and has developed some natural protection against their poison. Anyone else would be dead. To endure all that for her
30 country, which certainly didn't request it of her, must seem a bit mad to most people! There must be another reason.

American Lynne Cox swims in sub-zero temperatures through the planet's most inhospitable oceans wearing 35 only a swimsuit – for fun! According to Lynne, now in her forties, there is always something driving her on. She just has to do it. As a nine-year-old child she was rather fat, and she used to swim in an outdoor pool with the local youth club. One day a furious storm blew up, but she 40 refused to get out of the pool. Something made her carry on. Then she realised that, as the water got colder and rougher, she was actually getting faster and warmer, and she was really enjoying it. At the age of 14 she broke her first endurance record, one of many more to come. Years 45 later, experts discovered that Lynne has a totally even layer of body fat, like a seal. She is perfectly made for doing what she does, it seems.

The famous British explorer, Sir Ranulph Fiennes, has led many major expeditions (and has lost several fingers) 50 in the extreme cold, including walking right round the Arctic Circle, which took three years! He has also led expeditions in the extreme heat, and discovered the Lost City of Ubar in the Omani desert. It seems that many adventurers spend their lives trying to live up to the 55 image of a parent. Sir Ranulph's father was Commander of a regiment in the British Army, and died just before his son was born. Fiennes has said, 'If I am getting weak, I find a very powerful way of squashing it is to know that my father would have definitely done it.' 60

Adventurers are clearly different from the rest of us. There is probably no such thing as a 'normal' adventurer. Unsurprisingly, risk-takers tend to be single-minded and unusually determined people who hate the stability and routine that most people prefer. They tend to take risks 65 for the sheer 'fun' of it. The excitement becomes addictive, and they want more and more of it. Ordinary life seems boring in comparison. The famous sailor, Sir Robin Knox-Johnston says: 'Humans have been taking risks since we evolved. If something is difficult, almost impossible 70 to achieve, then it is worth doing.' Well, obviously. Could someone please pass me the TV remote control?

Vocabulary

Compound adjectives

1 Decide whether compound adjectives a–h describe personality (P) or appearance (A).

a bald-headed ....
b bad-tempered ....
c brown-eyed ....
d curly-haired ....
e easy-going ....
f long-legged ....
g rosy-cheeked ....
h suntanned ....

2 For each of the pairs in a–d, use one of the words below to form compound adjectives.

a warm-............
  broken-............
b absent-............
  broad-............
c ....-centred
  ....-disciplined
d big-............
  hard-............

3 Say which qualities in 2 are generally positive, negative or neutral.

> headed   hearted   minded   self

4 Give examples of how someone with the qualities in 2 might behave.

5 Can you name any famous people (real or fictional) that you think have the characteristics in 1 or 2?

Grammar

Relative clauses GR p171–172

1 Read sentences 1–8 below then answer questions a–g about them.

1 What was the name of the English explorer *who walked to the South Pole in 1912*?

2 In 1911, *when he was 42 years old*, Captain Robert Scott organised an expedition to the South Pole.

3 There were 33 people in Scott's expedition, *which set out on 1ˢᵗ June 1910*.

4 The men *who Scott took with him* were mostly army or naval officers.

5 The Norwegian explorer Amundsen, *whose party arrived at the South Pole a month earlier than Scott,* returned home safely.

6 When Scott arrived at the South Pole, he found a tent and a letter, *which Amundsen had left there for him*.

7 Scott and his men all died before they could reach the supply depot, *where they had left food and spare clothing.*

8 Scott had taken horses instead of dogs with him, *which most people agree was a big mistake.*

a In which sentences is the relative pronoun the subject of the verb in the relative clause?

b In which sentences is the relative the object of the verb in the relative clause?

c In which sentence can we leave out the relative pronoun?

d In which sentences can we use *that* instead of *who* or *which*?

e Which type of clause has commas immediately before the relative pronoun?

f In which sentence can we replace *who* with the more formal *whom*?

g In which sentence does the relative refer to the whole of the main clause?

2 **Join the pairs of sentences in a–e using *who* or *which*, adding commas where necessary and making any other changes.**

Example   The plasma TV has broken. I only bought it last week.

The plasma TV, which I only bought last week, has broken.

a That's the man. He's going to buy our house.

b I gave my daughter twenty euros. She spent it immediately.

c I live in a village called South Milton. It's a mile from the sea.

d Where are the sausages? Mum bought them on Saturday.

e Daniel Craig plays James Bond in *Casino Royale*. He also starred in the gangster film *Layer Cake*.

3 **Complete the sentences with *who, which, when, where* or *whose*, adding commas where necessary.**

Example   Harry is the guy _____ I met in Miyazaki _____ is a small town in Japan _____ we both taught English in the 1990s.

Harry is the guy *who* I met in Miyazaki, *which* is a small town in Japan *where* we both taught English in the 1990s.

a The shop _____ I usually get my groceries stays open until 10, _____ most other shops are shut.

b This chest of drawers _____ I inherited from my grandmother is 100 years old.

c Patricia is the girl _____ car we borrowed to go to that Spanish restaurant _____ they do great paella.

d Near my house is a park _____ there are some trees _____ my daughter loves climbing.

e The tall man _____ is standing over there is the cousin of the man _____ I introduced you to last night.

4 **Look again at your answers to 3. Decide for each one**

a if the relative pronoun could be omitted.

b if it would be possible to use *that* instead.

5 **Correct the mistakes in a–e. Sometimes more than one answer is possible.**

Example   Can you describe the man which you saw running out of the bank?

Can you describe the man *who* you saw running out of the bank?

a He's going to retire at 50, what I find surprising.

b Elvis Presley, that was probably the most famous pop star ever, died in 1977.

c Pam Fisher, who's older brother is a doctor, has also decided to study medicine.

d I got a letter this morning from my uncle Algernon who lives in Canada.

e The childminder looks after our children is ill today.

Listening

Part 2 Sentence completion

1 In pairs, tell each other about anything you collect now, or have collected in the past.

2 ◉)) You will hear an interview with a man called Alec Gardiner, who collects things. Read the **how to do it** box, then listen and complete sentences 1–10.

how to do it

Before you listen, you have 45 seconds to read the 10 sentences.

If you miss an answer, don't worry. Move on to the next sentence.

When you listen again, concentrate on the answers that you missed the first time.

Don't leave answers blank – make a guess.

1 Alec isn't exactly .... why he collects things.

2 Alec started collecting when he was ....

3 As a child Alec kept the things he collected in ....

4 Alec says it's a wonderful feeling when he completes a .... of something.

5 Alec likes collecting cartoon figures because they look .... and they amuse him.

6 It's possible to collect so many Mickey Mouse figures because Mickey is the .... cartoon character.

7 Alec keeps most of his cartoon figures in the living room on small ....

8 Alec used to buy things at collectors' .... and antique shops.

9 Alec doesn't like to leave the house for too long because he's afraid of ....

10 In order to complete a set of something, Alec sometimes has to pay out .... hundred pounds.

3 ◉)) Complete Alec's sentences a–e with the adjectives below. Listen again and check, then explain the difference between the –*ed* form and the –*ing* form of the adjectives.

> amazed/amazing   bored/boring
> interested/interesting   pleased/pleasing
> worried/worrying

a I was never .... as a child because there was always something new to collect.

b I became .... in more things and started collecting them as well.

c The most .... thing is when I find the last object to complete a set of something. That's really ....

d You'd be .... where Mickey turns up!

e Everything in there is precious, and I'm .... about burglaries.

4 In pairs, tell each other about

a something you are interested in.

b something you find boring.

c something you are pleased about.

d something you were amazed to find out.

Speaking

Part 2

1 In pairs, name as many objects in each photo as you can in two minutes. Compare your answers with another pair.

2 Match these adjectives with photos 1 or 2.

> bare   bright   clean   cluttered   cold   cosy
> (un)comfortable   dimly-lit   open-plan   relaxing   tidy

3 In pairs, brainstorm as many similarities and differences between the photos as you can and decide which are the most obvious. Use some of the phrases below to help you.

Similarities
- The most obvious similarity is that both photos show ....
- You can see .... in both photos.
- The room in photo 1 is .... Similarly, the room in photo 2 is ....
- The .... is/are the same in both photos.

Differences
- The biggest difference between the photos is that photo 1 shows .... whereas photo 2 shows ....
- While photo 1 shows .... , photo 2 on the other hand ....
- The .... is/are completely different in the two photos.

4 Describe the photos in detail. Say which room you prefer and why.

5 Discuss these questions.
a What kind of person do you think lives in each place?
b What sort of lifestyle do you think they might have?

Use of English

Part 4 Key word transformations

1 Read the **how to do it** box. Then look at the completed key word transformations in 1–4 and say which of these language areas is being tested in each.

> passives   phrasal verbs   relatives
> comparatives   adjectives   modal verbs

1   We didn't return to James' house until 11 p.m.

got

We finally <u>got back to</u> James' house at 11 p.m.

language area _____

2   They lost the box containing all the exam papers.

which

They lost the box <u>which contained</u> all the exam papers.

language area _____

3   Is Jason taller than Michael?

as

Is Michael <u>as tall as</u> Jason?

language area _____

4   They always opened his letters before he received them.

were

His letters <u>were always opened</u> before he received them.

language area _____

how to do it

Decide what the key word replaces. Remember it could be part of a phrase.

Read both sentences to check that they mean the same.

Check the number of words you have written. Remember that contractions, e.g. *isn't*, count as two words.

2 Rewrite each sentence a–g keeping the same meaning. Use two to five words, including the word given.

a   I haven't seen Harriet since February.

time

The last _____ in February.

b   It will be interesting to see if anybody can solve this problem.

interested

I _____ to see if anybody can solve this problem.

c   I'm sure Sam was there because he's in one of my photos.

must

Sam _____ because he's in one of my photos.

d   I won't tolerate his rude behaviour any more.

put

I _____ his rude behaviour any more.

e   This coffee isn't cool enough to drink.

too

This coffee _____ drink.

f   They cancelled the match because it was raining.

due

The match _____ rain.

g   I haven't got enough money to buy that MP3 player.

can't

I _____ buy that MP3 player.

Vocabulary

Body idioms

1 Label the parts of the body shown using these words.

ankle	calf	elbow	heel	hip
palm	shin	thigh	waist	wrist

2 Complete idioms a–h with these words, then match them with definitions 1–8.

arm	brains	eye	face	foot
hand	leg	tongue		

a keep an .... on someone/something
b twist someone's ....
c pull someone's ....
d put your .... in it
e be on the tip of your ....
f give someone a ....
g keep a straight ....
h pick someone's ....

1 persuade or force someone to do something
2 find out about something from someone who knows more about it than you
3 watch someone/something carefully
4 help someone
5 play a joke on someone by making them believe something that isn't true
6 say or do something wrong, foolish or embarrassing
7 be something almost remembered or recalled, but not quite
8 manage not to laugh or smile at something you find funny

3 Tell a partner about a situation when
a you couldn't keep a straight face.
b someone pulled your leg.
c you put your foot in it.
d you twisted someone's arm.
e you picked someone's brains.
f somebody gave you a hand.

1 ....   2 ....
3 ....
4 ....
5 ....

6 ....
7 ....
8 ....
9 ....   10 ....

Writing

Part 1 A letter

1 Read the exam task below. Are you asked to write a, b or c?

a a letter requesting information

b a letter of application

c a letter of complaint

> You have seen this advertisement in a magazine and you want to organise a weekend for you and six friends. One of your friends is only 17. Read the advertisement and the notes you have made. Then write a letter to Adrenalin Adventure asking for more details.

2 Decide whether your letter should letter be formal or informal.

3 Put a–f into the paragraph plan below, with the two most important queries before the less important ones.

a ask about dates

b ask about accommodation

c say where you saw the advertisement

d ask about age limits

e say who you are and why you are writing

f ask about cost

Paragraph 1

- ....
- ....

Paragraph 2

- ....
- ....

Paragraph 3

- ....
- ....

ADRENALIN ADVENTURE

Escape the daily grind for two days on one of our Adrenalin Adventure Weekends.

Activities: choose two from: kayaking, hill-walking, surfing, wind-surfing, mountain-biking, climbing*, horse-riding**

* experienced climbers only
** £20 supplement applies

— single rooms?

Accommodation: our three wooden lodges sleep 12 people each

— includes meals and hire of equipment?

Cost: £199 per person

Dates: weekends in July and August
— places available on 12–13 August?

We welcome individuals and groups (adults only).

— lower age limit?

Adrenalin Adventure, Newquay, Cornwall NQ77 5TG

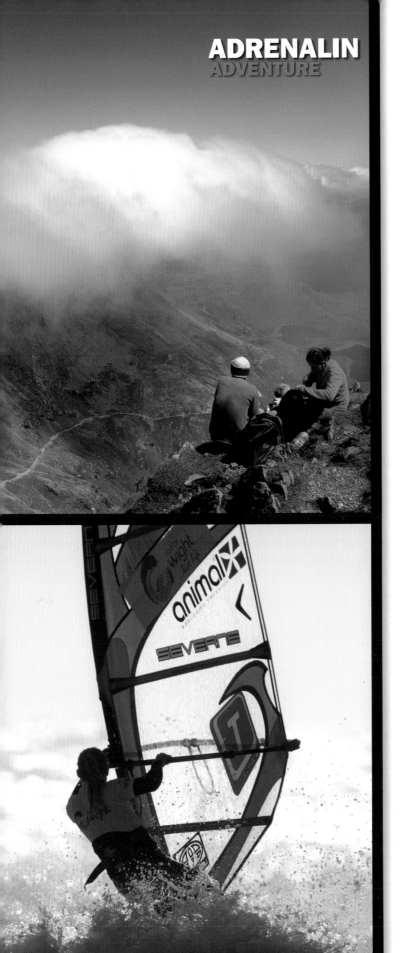

ADRENALIN
ADVENTURE

4 Read the phrases in the language box below and complete them with a–f.

a could   d please
b grateful   e wonder
c have   f would

●●● Polite requests

Could you .... let me know ... ?	
I'd be .... if you could tell me ...	
I .... if you could inform me ... ?	
.... you possibly give me some information about ... ?	
Could I .... some details about .. ?	
.... it be possible to ... ?	

5 Complete polite requests a–f using the phrases in the language box to help you.

a .... have some information about your adventure holidays?

b .... send me a brochure?

c .... about the cost of the holiday?

d .... could let me know if there are any places left on the skiing course.

e .... how much it costs to hire equipment?

f .... if you could send me some information about accommodation.

6 Look at the notes you have made on the advert and do the following.

a Decide which paragraph they fit into.

b Write them as complete questions, using the polite requests and the sequencing words *firstly, secondly, thirdly, finally*, as in the example.

Example   Firstly, I'd be grateful if you could let me know if there are any places available on 12th and 13th August.

7 Write the letter in 1 using all your notes.

Review

1 Complete sentences a–g with compound adjectives.

a My brother is really absent-................ . He's always forgetting and losing things.

b 'You're looking very sun................ , George. Have you been on holiday?' 'Yes' I've just spent two weeks in the south of Italy.'

c Melissa was extremely fond of her cat, so she was ....-hearted when it died.

d Geoff goes on and on about getting the top mark in his exam. He's so big-................ !

e 'I didn't think Harry was ....-tempered.' 'He may seem easy-going to you but he gets angry at the slightest thing.'

f Sam is too ....-centred to talk to people he thinks are unimportant or not useful to him.

g Cathy finds ....-headed men attractive, maybe it's because her dad lost his hair at an early age.

2 Complete the idioms in sentences a–h with these parts of the body.

arm	brains	eye	face	foot
hand	leg	tongue		

a 'Would you like another piece of chocolate?' 'Oh, go on then. If you twist my ....'

b David really put his .... in it when he asked Samantha how Steve was getting on. They split up three months ago!

c 'I'm having problems with my PC. You know all about computers, don't you? Can I pick your .... ?'

d 'John told me that you were moving to New York.' 'New York! No, he was just pulling your ....'

e 'What's the French for 'lawn'? It'll come to me in a moment. It's on the tip of my ....'

f 'I've got to carry these chairs upstairs.' 'I'll give you a(n) ....'

g We couldn't keep a straight .... when the head teacher nodded off during the lesson.

h Can you keep a(n) .... on the children for me while I'm out?

3 Complete the text with the correct verbs below (a, b or c) in –ing or –ed form.

A 15-year-old girl has just pulled off an (1) .... achievement, by walking 200 miles across the Arctic wilderness of Baffin Island. Alicia Hempleman-Adams faced (2) .... challenges as she crossed mountain peaks, glaciers and steep-sided fjords. Her father had travelled the same route himself and at first the prospect of his young daughter following in his footsteps was (3) .... Because of her age, he felt (4) .... that she would find it too (5) .... He was also (6) .... that she could get frost-bite. Alicia, however, was (7) .... that she could do it, and she's been proved right. Though very (8) .... by the end she was (9) .... to achieve her goal.

1	a	amaze	b	annoy	c	entertain
2	a	concern	b	terrify	c	bore
3	a	horrify	b	entertain	c	amuse
4	a	confuse	b	satisfy	c	worry
5	a	embarrass	b	excite	c	exhaust
6	a	interest	b	concern	c	amuse
7	a	convince	b	please	c	entertain
8	a	bore	b	tire	c	relax
9	a	thrill	b	confuse	c	encourage

All in the mind

Lead in

1 ◗) Look at photos 1–6 and listen to the people introducing themselves. Try to remember their names and what they say, but don't make any notes.

2 Which of a–g are you likely to remember easily? What could make them easy or hard to remember?

 a a phone number
 b a tune
 c English vocabulary
 d the steps of a dance
 e the clothes that somebody was wearing on a certain occasion
 f how to get to a place you've only visited once
 g the date of a friend's birthday

3 Do the quiz below then turn to page 153 to find out what your answers say about your learning style.

What's your **learning style**?

1 When you spell a difficult word in English, do you
 A try to see the word in your head?
 B say the word, either aloud or in your head?
 C write the word down to find out what feels right?

2 When you chat socially with other people, do you
 A use as few words as possible?
 B enjoy talking and listening?
 C use your hands a lot?

3 When you are trying to concentrate, are you distracted most by
 A untidiness?
 B sounds?
 C movement?

4 When you meet somebody again, having met them only once before, are you most likely to
 A forget their name but remember their face and where you met?
 B remember their name and what you talked about, but forget where you met them?
 C remember best what you did together?

5 When you read for pleasure, do you prefer
 A descriptions?
 B dialogue?
 C action?

6 When you learn to do something new, do you prefer
 A seeing a demonstration and a picture?
 B listening to verbal instructions?
 C trying by yourself first?

7 When you're learning how to use new computer software, do you
 A try to find diagrams and charts?
 B ask help from someone who knows the software?
 C keep experimenting until you've learnt how to use it?

4 Turn to page 154 and do part 2 of the Memory Test in 1.

Reading

Part 2 Gapped text

1 Try to answer these questions without using a clock, calculator, ruler or any other device. Are they easy, difficult or impossible?

a How wide is the door of the room you're in, to the nearest millimetre?

b What is the time to the nearest second?

c What day of the week was 1st June 1768?

d What is 7,623 x 4,592?

2 Read the magazine article opposite quickly and find the name of

a a film character who can do amazing calculations in his head.

b the real person that the character is based on.

c the scientist who thinks that we all have the potential to do these things.

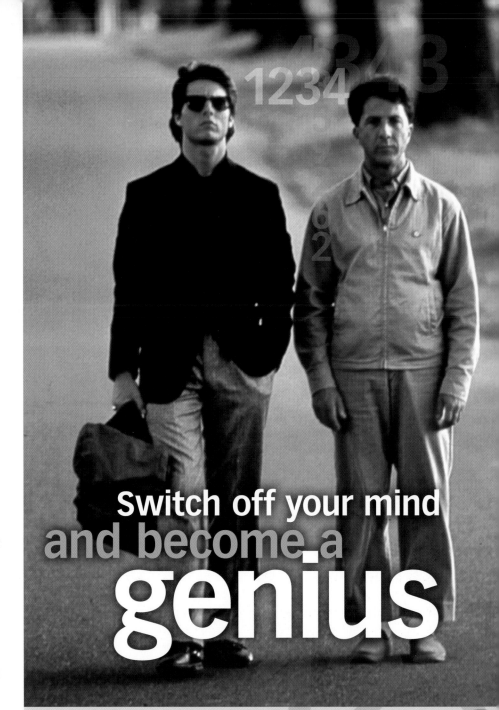

Switch off your mind and become a genius

Doctor	Do you know how much 312 times 123 is?
Ray	*(without hesitation)* 38,376.
Charlie	*(doing the sum on a calculator)* He's right.
Doctor	What?
05 **Charlie**	He's right!
Doctor	He's right!
Charlie	Yes. Ray, how much is 4,343 times 1,234?
Ray	*(without hesitation)* 5,359,262.
Charlie	He's a genius!

10 These lines are from a film called *Rain Man*, starring Tom Cruise and Dustin Hoffman. Charlie Babbitt's brother, Ray, lives in a home because he is unable to work or look after himself. **1** ☐ For example, he can perform very complex mental arithmetic with astonishing speed and accuracy. Ray is a 'savant': somebody who has 15 specific, extraordinary abilities, but who is incapable of most everyday tasks.

Ray Babbitt's character is based on a real savant called Kim Peek, who was born in 1951 with an unusually formed brain. Doctors predicted that Kim would never be able to lead a normal life, and it is
20 true that he still lives with his father, who looks after him. As a child, he couldn't walk until he was four years old. However, he has always had extraordinary mental abilities. He could use a dictionary when he was three years old. **2**☐ Since childhood, he has
25 read, and can recall in detail, about 7,600 books. He can read two pages simultaneously (one with each eye) in about 10 seconds and remember forever what he has read.

Savants are very rare: there are only about 25 alive
30 in the world today. Their special abilities differ. The blind American savant, Leslie Lemke, was able to play Tchaikovsky's Piano Concerto No 1 after hearing it once, even though he had never had a piano lesson. **3**☐ Other talents have included being able
35 to measure exact distances with the naked eye and knowing the exact time without looking at a clock.

Daniel Tammet is a British savant and
40 his special abilities are mathematical and linguistic. (He managed to learn Icelandic in a few
45 days, and could speak it fluently after one week.) Unlike most savants, Tammet is a good communicator. **4**☐ He explains that his mathematical feats – like
50 reciting pi to 22,514 decimal places – do not involve 'thinking'. **5**☐ For Daniel, numbers are not abstract, they are real and familiar, like friends.

Intriguingly, some scientists believe that we all have these kinds of amazing abilities hidden deep
55 inside our brains, but that we lose them as our brains develop. **6**☐ This theory is supported by the fact that, very occasionally, people acquire these abilities in adult life as the result of brain damage. Allan Snyder, director of the Australian
60 Centre for the Mind, believes that we all might be able to release special skills by somehow 'switching off' the normal, conscious functions of the mind. He conducts experiments on himself, firing strong magnetic waves into his head to see whether he
65 can temporarily become a savant. **7**☐ 'We are all potential geniuses,' he claims.

3 Read the article again carefully, then choose from the sentences A–H the one which fits each gap (1–7). There is one extra sentence.

A The British savant Stephen Wiltshire managed to draw a highly accurate picture of the London skyline after a single helicopter trip over the city.

B Although finding volunteers for his experiments can be difficult, as Snyder admits, he believes that the possibilities are very exciting.

C By the age of four and a half, he had memorised the first eight volumes of an encyclopaedia.

D He can reflect on his own special abilities in a way that most savants cannot.

E However, as Charlie discovers, Ray has a few incredible abilities.

F They all have a similar ability to do amazing calculations in their head, like Ray Babbitt in the film *Rain Man*.

G Instead, he visualises the number in his head, as if he's watching a film.

H Savants are different: they don't develop normally and as a result they don't lose their special abilities.

4 Find words or phrases in the article that mean

a immediately (lines 1–9)
b very, very quickly (lines 10–15)
c at the same time (lines 16–28)
d quickly and without mistakes (lines 37–52)
e sometimes, but not very often (lines 53–66)
f for a short time (lines 53–66)

5 Which of the special abilities mentioned in the article would you most like to have? How would you use it?

Vocabulary

Mental activities

1 Match a–j with 1–10 to form definitions of the verbs in italics.

a If you *suspect* something is true …
b If you *consider* someone to be attractive …
c If you *doubt* something that you've heard …
d If you *recollect* an experience …
e If you *contemplate* your future …
f If you *analyse* a problem …
g If you *memorise* a number …
h If you can't *comprehend* something …
i If somebody *reminds* you of another person …
j If an idea *occurs* to you …

1 you think about it in a logical way.
2 you think it probably isn't true.
3 you learn it so that you won't forget it.
4 that is your opinion.
5 they make you think of that other person.
6 you think about it for quite a long time.
7 it comes into your mind suddenly.
8 you think it might be true but you aren't sure.
9 you don't understand it.
10 you think about it at a later date.

2 Choose the correct verbs in italics to complete a–e.

a I often sit and *contemplate/recollect* the meaning of life, but I *doubt/suspect* I'll ever find any answers!
b It *reminded/occurred* to me last night that I usually like people who *remind/recollect* me of my parents.
c Until then, she had always *considered/contemplated* him a very logical person who could *analyse/contemplate* any situation.
d She says that she has *recollected/memorised* 10,000 telephone numbers, but I strongly *suspect/doubt* that she's lying.
e I *recollect/memorise* seeing snow for the first time when I was three years old; I couldn't *consider/comprehend* what was happening.

Grammar

Comparatives and superlatives
GR p172–173

1 Read sentences 1–8 below. In pairs decide

a which sentences contain comparatives and which contain superlatives.
b which sentences you agree with and which you disagree with.

1 Women communicate *far better than* men.
2 *The more attractive* you are, *the easier* it is to make friends.
3 *The funniest* comedian ever is Steve Martin.
4 *The most intelligent* people are often *the least talkative.*
5 *The more* you study a language, *the harder* it gets.
6 Humans are becoming *more and more dependent* on machines.
7 Teenagers don't work *as hard as* adults.
8 People are usually *more attractive than* they think.

2 Rewrite sentences a–f, keeping the same meaning, but using another form of comparative.

Example   I'm worse at remembering faces than I am at remembering names.

I'm not as good at remembering faces as I am at remembering names.

a My best friend drives more slowly than I do.
b The weather is cooler in the autumn.
c Air tickets are getting less and less expensive.
d In my opinion, this exercise isn't as easy as it looks.
e This school isn't as big as I remember it.
f Our local shops are further than we'd like them to be.

3 In pairs, make comparisons about the photos in 1–3 using the adjectives given or your own ideas.

Example   I don't think a footballer is as athletic as a ballerina.

I don't agree. I think a footballer is more athletic, but far less graceful.

4 Complete these sentences in an appropriate way.

a The richer people become, …

b The better I got to know him, …

c The colder the weather becomes, …

d The more we use cars rather than public transport …

e … , the more tired I get.

5 Complete sentences 1–6 with the superlative form of the adjective in brackets and the correct option (A, B or C). Check the answers on page 154.

1 The (high) mountain in the world is … .
A Everest B K2 C Kangchenjunga

2 The (far) of these planets from the sun is … .
A Neptune B Uranus C Pluto

3 The (dangerous) job in Britain is being a … .
A builder B fisherman C policeman

4 The (hard) substance in the world is … .
A diamond B steel C glass

5 The (large) creature to live on earth is the … .
A blue whale B brontosaurus C elephant

6 The (intelligent) animal on earth is the … .
A dolphin B dog C chimpanzee

6 Use the prompts in a–e to write superlative questions with *most* or *least*. Then ask and answer in pairs as in the example.

Example frightening experience/have

What's the most frightening experience you've ever had?

It was when my brother put a spider in my bed.

a dangerous thing/do

b interesting place/visit

c attractive person/meet

d expensive present/buy

e enjoyable film/see

1 athletic graceful rich

2 exciting enjoyable safe

3 healthy expensive tasty

Listening

Part 3 Multiple matching

1 Look at pictures 1–3. In your opinion, which one best conveys the feeling of being in a dream?

2 Discuss how dreams can be different from real life. Think about
   • people and places   • sequence of events   • feelings   • time

3 ◉) You will hear five people talking about their dreams. Choose from the list A–F the things that each person dreams about. Use the letters only once. There is one extra letter.

A things going wrong	Speaker 1	☐ 1
B animals	Speaker 2	☐ 2
C ordinary, everyday events	Speaker 3	☐ 3
D unconnected events	Speaker 4	☐ 4
E very recent events	Speaker 5	☐ 5
F strangers		

4 ◉) Complete the verb + preposition expressions that the speakers use. Then listen again and check your answers.

Speaker 1   I sometimes *make* .... more interesting dreams.
Speaker 2   Things normally *work* .... better in my dreams.
Speaker 3   I know I'm *messing* things .... , but I can't help it.
Speaker 4   If I *came* .... somebody from my dream, I'd be terrified.
Speaker 5   My brother is always *going* .... about his dreams.

5 Replace each verb + preposition expression in 4 with a single verb.

6 Discuss these questions.

   a Do you analyse your dreams? What do you think some of them might mean?

   b Have any of your dreams ever come true?

Speaking

Part 2

1 Look at the list below of ten phobias, things people are afraid of, and answer these questions.

   a Which do you think people fear about each one?

   b Which can you match to photos 1 and 2?

heights	small spaces
flying	public speaking
open spaces	darkness
spiders	germs and dirt
thunderstorms	water

2 Match a–h with photo 1 or photo 2. Brainstorm other words you might need to describe the photos.

   a ropes

   b depth

   c mask

   d cave

   e torch

   f rockface

   g wet-suit

   h darkness

3 Compare the photos and say why these activities would be enjoyable for some people but a nightmare for others. The phrases below and the **how to do it** box will help you.

●●● Comparing photos

In the first photo … but in the second one …
This picture … while on the other hand this one …
In comparison to the first photo, this one …

how to do it

Describe each scene in general. Mention any obvious similarities or differences.

Say how they make you feel, or what they remind you of.

Describe what the people are doing and wearing.

Say how the people might be feeling and how you might feel in a similar situation.

Use of English

Part 3 Word formation

●●● noun suffixes

We can add suffixes to verbs or adjectives to make nouns. Sometimes the spelling changes.

verb	→	noun
express	**-(t)ion**	expression
dominate		domination
manage	**-ment**	management
excite		excitement

adjective	→	noun
happy	**-ness**	happiness
weak		weakness
similar	**-ity**	similarity
popular		popularity

1 Add a suffix to each of the underlined words in a–g to make a noun that completes the second sentence.

Example   They <u>donated</u> a lot of money to Oxfam.

They made a big <u>donation</u> to Oxfam.

a My boss thinks it's very important to be <u>punctual</u>.
My boss thinks _____ is very important.

b The police are <u>investigating</u> the crime.
The police are carrying out an _____ into the crime.

c My secretary has resigned. I need to find someone to <u>replace</u> her.
My secretary has resigned. I need to find a _____ for her.

d Unlike many superstars, she's well known for being <u>polite</u>.
Unlike many superstars, she's well known for her _____ .

e My brother is very <u>sensitive</u> to other people's feelings.
My brother shows a great deal of _____ to other people's feelings.

f Do you <u>enjoy</u> watching reality TV shows?
Do you get a lot of _____ from watching reality TV shows?

g Mick is <u>responsible</u> for organising the Christmas party.
Mick has _____ for organising the Christmas party.

Are geniuses born or made?

Most people consider that geniuses are different from ordinary people from birth. However, a **0** *psychologist* called Professor Michael Howe has challenged this **1** _____. According to him, the secret of genius is hard work!

Professor Howe has also shown that nearly all geniuses have the **2** _____ to concentrate for long periods of time. They are not easily distracted by people or events because it is so **3** _____ for them to achieve their goal. 'What makes geniuses **4** _____ is their long-term **5** _____,' he explains. 'All geniuses have a clear idea of their goal, and they pursue that goal with total **6** _____. Their **7** _____ are exceptional because they make an exceptional effort.'

Throughout the centuries, the **8** _____ composers in the world have often been child prodigies. However, even the most exceptionally able still took at least ten years of hard study to become a major composer.

It would be untrue to suggest that every genius begins as a child prodigy. Many **9** _____ talented adults – including Charles Darwin – were unexceptional in their youth. And what's more, many child prodigies do not go on to achieve anything **10** _____ as adults.

2 Read the text opposite, ignoring the gaps, and say whether a–c are true or false according to the text.

a Michael Howe believes that all geniuses are naturally clever.

b Even the best composers had to work hard to become great.

c All geniuses are very clever as children.

3 Complete the gaps in the text with words formed from 1–10 as shown.

Example   psychology → *noun (a person)*

psychologist

1 believe → *noun*
2 able → *noun*
3 importance → *adjective*
4 difference → *adjective*
5 commit → *noun*
6 dedicate → *noun*
7 achieve → *noun*
8 great → *superlative form*
9 high → *adverb*
10 significance → *adjective*

Vocabulary

Expressions with *mind*

1 Look at expressions a–l and say in which ones *mind* is a verb, and in which a noun.

a mind your own business	g spring to mind
b Do you mind if …	h take your mind off something
c I don't mind + noun or –*ing*	i be bored out of your mind
d change your mind	j be in two minds about something
e make up your mind	k bear something in mind
f mind your head	l Would you mind + –*ing*

2 Use expressions from 1 in the correct form to complete what the people are saying or thinking in 1–4.

1 I'm ....

2 I hope you haven't ....
.... ?

3 Would you ....
.... ?

4 This film will ....
.... our problems.

3 Rewrite these sentences using an expression with *mind* from 1.

a As she watched the plane land, she suddenly remembered her own first experience of air travel.

b I can't decide which restaurant to go to this evening.

c Please could you open the door for me?

d My dad is happy to give us a lift into town.

e I don't want advice about my personal life. Please don't interfere.

f Is it all right if I give my friend your phone number?

Writing

Part 1 A letter

tip Write one paragraph for each main idea. Don't write more than four paragraphs.

1 Read the letter of application below. In which paragraph does the writer

a   say what else she is sending with the letter?

b   say how good her English is, and how she'd like to improve it?

c   give details of her qualifications?

d   say where she saw the advertisement and why she is writing?

2 Raquel starts the letter with *Dear Ms Jordan* and finishes with *Yours sincerely*. If she didn't know the name of the recipient, how would she

a   start the letter?

b   finish the letter?

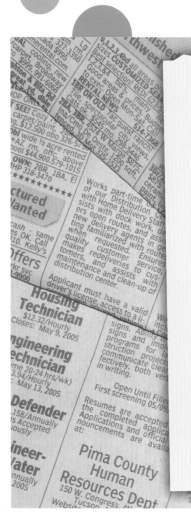

Dear Ms Jordan,

I am writing in response to your advertisement in the *Daily News* for the Post-Graduate Diploma in English Literature. I want to apply for a place on the course that starts on 15th September.

I am 22 years old and have just done a degree in English Language and Literature at Madrid University, which I passed with Distinction. While at university I specialised in 19th century literature. Now I would very much like to increase my knowledge of 20th century literature.

I have visited Britain a few times and went to summer language schools in Brighton and Oxford. I can read and write English very well, and I am keen to continue my studies in Britain to improve my speaking and listening skills.

Here's my CV with lots of information about my qualifications and work experience. I look forward to getting a reply.

Yours sincerely

Raquel Gonzalez

enc. CV

3 Identify seven words or phrases in Raquel's letter that are too informal or inappropriate for a letter of application. Replace them with a–g.

a completed	d on a number of occasions	g full details of
b I enclose	e hearing from you	
c attended	f I would like to	

4 Match a–f with 1–6 to form sentences appropriate for a formal letter.

a   I look forward to hearing from you   1   ... , I have a degree in English.
b   As for my qualifications   2   ... working in hotels.
c   I'd be grateful if you could   3   ... send me details of the syllabus.
d   I should like to apply for   4   ... at your earliest convenience.
e   I have two years' experience of   5   ... for interview from 1st March.
f   I am available   6   ... the post of receptionist.

5 You saw this advertisement in a newspaper. Read the advertisement and your notes, then write a letter of application in 120–150 words.

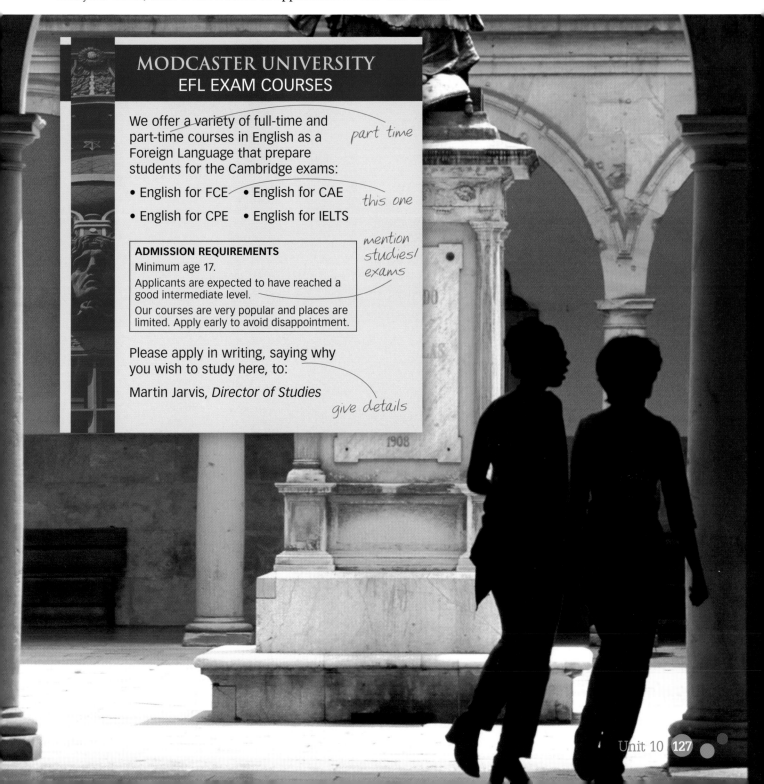

Review

1 Rewrite sentences a–i using the verbs in the box in the correct form, and making any other necessary changes to the sentences.

~~suspect~~	consider	memorise	remind
analyse	contemplate	occur	
comprehend	doubt	recollect	

Example
I've always thought that he didn't like me.
I've always suspected that he didn't like me.

a John makes me think of a friend I had at school.

b I don't think we will win the World Cup.

c In my opinion, he's very impolite.

d For homework my daughter had to learn a Shakespeare poem by heart.

e He's thinking carefully about resigning and looking for another job.

f We need to think logically about the results of the experiment.

g Can you remember exactly what he said?

h I suddenly thought of the answer in the bath.

i It's difficult to understand why she wants a divorce.

2 Form the part of speech shown in brackets from the words in a–h.

a astonish (noun)   e illegality (adjective)

b discussion (verb)   f sad (noun)

c inform (noun)   g carelessness (adjective)

d excitement (verb)   h similar (noun)

3 Use the correct form of words in 2 to complete these sentences.

a Liam and I had a long .... about the advantages and disadvantages of living abroad.

b It was very .... of David to lose the house keys.

c The police rang to .... me that they'd caught the man who stole my car.

d Harry bears a striking .... to his brother. It's sometimes difficult to tell them apart.

e In Britain it's .... to sell cigarettes to people under 16.

f It was with great .... that doctors announced the death of the much-loved President.

g Mark is incredibly forgetful. It would .... me if he remembered his mother's birthday.

h The news that a circus was coming to town caused great .... among the children.

4 Complete the text below using words formed from the base words in 1–10.

0	regular	4	difficult	8	surprise
1	invite	5	sincere	9	equal
2	arrange	6	commit	10	sense
3	psychology	7	participate		

Why do we over-commit?

Most people **(0)** *regularly* over-commit. How often do we agree to meet friends, accept **(1)** ...., or offer to help a family member, only to realise that in making the **(2)** .... we've been too generous with our time? **(3)** .... believe that we 'over-commit' because we have **(4)** .... judging how much time there is available. We fill our diaries with things to do, **(5)** .... believing that we'll have more time in the future than we have in the present. Of course, when tomorrow turns into today, we discover that we are too busy to fulfil all of the **(6)** .... that we've made. The nature of time deceives us and we 'forget' about how things fill our days and compete for our time. Nearly all the **(7)** .... in a survey believed that they would have more free time next month than now. When questioned a month later, they were **(8)** .... to find that they were **(9)** .... busy. So next time a distant cousin suggests a get-together, or you are invited to three parties in the week before Christmas, try to think ahead and consider whether it would be more **(10)** .... to be less generous with your time.

Man and machine ¹¹

Lead in

1 In pairs, look at the photos and discuss these questions.

  a What benefits have these inventions brought?

  b What problems have they caused?

2 Do the quiz opposite. Then compare answers and check your score on page 154.

3 Think about these questions, then discuss your ideas.

  a Why do boys seem to be more interested in technology than girls?

  b Do you think that technology can solve these problems? If so, how? If not, why not?

   • global warming

   • famine

   • disease

ARE YOU A TECHNOPHILE OR TECHNOPHOBE?

1 If you were buying a new car, and had to choose between two similar models, would you

  a carefully compare all technical details and specifications?

  b want to know only the most important differences, like engine size or fuel consumption?

  c just buy the colour you liked best?

2 'Most of the world's problems can be solved by science and technology.' Is this statement

  a true?

  b partially true?

  c false?

3 How would you react if you switched on an electrical appliance and it didn't work?

  a I'd check the fuse in the plug, then look in the manual.

  b I'd press a few buttons to see if I could make it work.

  c I'd get someone else to help.

4 What kind of mobile have you got?

  a One with all the latest features.

  b One that just allows you to make calls and send texts.

  c I don't know./I haven't got a mobile.

5 Imagine you want to buy a new TV. Do you

  a buy the most up to date model

  b wait and buy the most up to date model once it has come down in price

  c buy an old end-of-line model

6 Do you buy goods online

  a more than once a week?

  b about once a month?

  c hardly ever or never?

Reading

1 In the following conversation, one of the speakers is human, and one is a computer called 'Jabberwacky'. Can you say which is which? Give reasons for your opinion.

How are you today?

Fine, what about you?

I'm OK thanks. I'm a bit tired.

Did you sleep well last night?

No, not really.

Why not?

I drank too much coffee.

What did you do today?

Nothing much. Had breakfast.

What did you eat for breakfast?

Toast and coffee.

Toast is awesome.

Yes. Did you have toast for breakfast?

Does French toast count?

Yes.

How so?

Well, it's bread with egg. But it's fried not toasted.

Yes, I know. That's why I wanted you to explain it to me.

2 Read the text opposite about a competition to design intelligent computers, and say which of these statements is true, according to the text.

   a Scientists have already created computers that can communicate exactly like humans.

   b Scientists may be able to make a computer that communicates like humans but it won't happen for a long time.

   c Scientists will never be able to make a computer that communicates like humans.

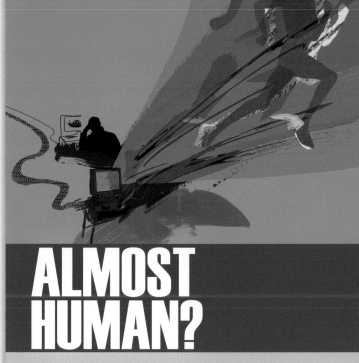

ALMOST HUMAN?

Steven Spielberg's 2001 film A.I. is the story of David, a robot-boy who can think and feel like a human. The film is set in the distant future, but the idea is not as far-fetched as it may seem at first. Today
5 scientists are developing computers that are capable of interacting and communicating with humans.

It all started in 1950 when the British mathematician Alan Turing, who had famously helped to break German military codes during the Second World
10 War, asked how scientists would know whether computers had successfully achieved truly artificial intelligence. His suggestion was that, in order for a computer to be described as truly intelligent, it had to give replies in a conversation which could not be
15 distinguished from a human's replies.

New Yorker Hugh Loebner was fascinated by the idea of artificial intelligence, and in the early 1990s offered $100,000 to the first program to pass the 'Turing Test', that is, to successfully fool a panel of judges into
20 thinking it was a real person. That challenge has turned into an annual competition, but despite 16 years of trying, no technology has made that breakthrough, and the grand prize remains unclaimed.

However, every year the judges award a prize to the
25 computer program that comes closest to passing the test, and in 2006 the lucky winner was Joan. She is just a few years old but is already very talkative. Joan's maker, the British entrepreneur Rollo Carpenter, emerged victorious after a day of
30 intense competition as a quartet of software experts and their creations battled it out in a blind test held at University College London. The judges held typed conversations – similar to an Internet chat program – with all four of the challengers, before they declared
35 Joan the world's most human computer program.

3 Read the text again carefully, and for questions 1–8, choose the answer (A, B, C or D) which you think fits best according to the text.

1 Robots such as David in Spielberg's film *A.I.*
   A are completely unrealistic.
   B already exist.
   C could conceivably exist in the future.
   D are being developed by scientists.

2 According to Alan Turing, what would a computer that could think for itself be able to do?
   A answer questions
   B win the Hugh Loebner competition
   C break military codes
   D take part in a conversation with you and make you think it was human

3 When did the Loebner competition begin?
   A in the Second World War
   B about 16 years ago
   C in the 1950s
   D before computer programs were invented

4 How many computer programs took part in the competition this year?
   A Joan and two others
   B Joan and three others
   C Joan and four others
   D Joan and five others

5 What was the result of the competition?
   A Joan won the $100,000 prize.
   B Joan won the competition for the second time.
   C Joan was considered the most human of the four competitors.
   D None of the competitors was good enough to win a prize.

6 According to the text, what is unusual about the technology behind Joan?
   A Its store of responses grows larger as it interacts with humans.
   B It drives a number of programs that have won the competition.
   C It's much better than its rivals.
   D Its name, 'Jabberwacky'.

7 Joan's maker, Rollo Carpenter, is happy with the result because
   A the test was subjective.
   B he thinks people will believe that Joan is human.
   C he won a lot of money.
   D he has got a job working with call centre companies.

8 What is the experts' view of artificial intelligence?
   A Carpenter's computer is too basic.
   B Robots will replace human workers in call centres.
   C Carpenter will definitely win the competition in the future.
   D Nobody will win the Loebner competition in the near future.

4 Match a–e with 1–5 to make verb–noun collocations. Then check your answers by finding them in the text.

a	pass	1	a prize
b	make	2	a conversation
c	award	3	a competition
d	hold	4	a test
e	enter	5	a breakthrough

The victory earned Carpenter a $2,000 prize and a bronze medal – and also helped him retain the title he first won last year for the first time with a computer program called George. Both Joan and George are based
40 on technology that Carpenter has named 'Jabberwacky'. What's unusual about Jabberwacky is that it uses its experience of interaction with humans to create a store from which to draw its next response. The Jabberwacky system has entered the competition every year since
45 2003, and now seems to be building up an impressive lead over its rivals. That may be helped by the fact that it is always able to enlarge its database through conversations online.

'I'm very pleased,' said Carpenter. 'In a way this is a
50 very subjective test ... but I believe that for practical purposes, people will believe Joan is a human.'

Carpenter has already identified a possible role for computers like Joan. He is working with call centre companies to help train his robots to understand how
55 better to interact with humans, with the possibility of using them to replace human workers in the near future – a prospect that fills many people with horror.

However, experts say that a program that will successfully pass the Turing test and scoop the
60 $100,000 prize is still some years away. 'We're still a long way off, but I think Rollo Carpenter is onto something,' said Duncan Graham-Rowe, one of the judges. Carpenter is not put off, being used to the long haul. The very first version of the program was written
65 in 1982, and ran on a Sinclair ZX81, a primitive home computer which had a maximum of 16K of RAM!

Vocabulary

Gadgets and their parts

1 Read the advertisement below, then complete gaps 1–6 with these words.

| battery life | Internet access | ringtones | wireless | text |

3G NOKSUNG 4470

Chat to friends, ¹_____ them, or send picture messages with Noksung's latest 3G mobile.

- With ²_____ you can send and receive emails on your phone and ³_____ the web.

- Over 50 ⁴_____ to choose from – from a simple bell to a clip from a Top 20 single.

- The keypad is easy to use and has voice-activated dialling.

- Great ⁵_____ – you can get at least 80 hours of use.

- Make and receive calls while you are on the move using the ⁶_____ headset.

- Includes high-resolution digital camera.

2 Write an advertisement for this MP3 player. Use the advert in 1 as a model, and make it sound as attractive as possible.

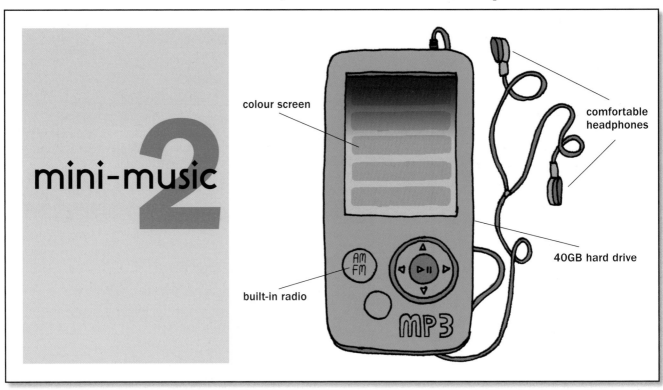

mini-music 2

colour screen

comfortable headphones

40GB hard drive

built-in radio

Grammar

Conditionals GR p174–175

1 Correct the mistakes in the underlined clauses in a–d and name the type of conditional (zero, 1st, 2nd or 3rd).

a <u>If I would win the lottery</u>, I'd buy an enormous plasma television.

b If you give me a blank CD, <u>I burn the album onto it for you</u>.

c <u>If you'll press this key</u>, it sends the text message.

d <u>If I knew it was illegal</u>, I wouldn't have downloaded all those songs.

2 In pairs, decide if future events a–f are probable or improbable for your partner. Then, depending on your decision, write a question for each one using the first or second conditional.

Example   go out this evening

Improbable – Where would you go if you went out this evening?

Probable – Where will you go if you go out this evening?

a win the lottery

b go to the cinema at the weekend

c visit the UK this summer

d surf the Internet at the weekend

e lose your mobile phone

f not have any homework this evening

3 In the same pairs, ask and answer the questions you wrote in 2.

4 Write sentences using the third conditional as in the example.

Example   I missed the bus so I was late for my class.

If I hadn't missed the bus, I wouldn't have been late for my class.

a I bought a new MP3 player because I lost my old one.

b I didn't know you liked opera, so I didn't buy you a ticket.

c The burglar got in because I forgot to shut the window.

d Carl didn't buy the computer because it was so expensive.

e I couldn't find your number so I couldn't phone you.

5 Read mixed conditional sentences 1–4 and answer questions a–d below.

1 If Jane didn't have a cold, she'd go swimming with Tom.

2 If Jane didn't have a cold, she'd have gone swimming with Tom.

3 If Josh hadn't spent all his money, he'd have gone out with his friends.

4 If Josh hadn't spent all his money, he'd go out with his friends.

a Does Jane have a cold in sentence 1, sentence 2 or both?

b Has Tom already gone swimming in sentence 1, sentence 2 or both?

c Has Josh spent all his money in sentence 3, sentence 4 or both?

d Have his friends gone out in sentence 3, sentence 4 or both?

6 Complete sentences a–f with mixed conditionals.

Example   Harry didn't go to the party because he's getting up early tomorrow.

Harry would have gone to the party if he weren't getting up early tomorrow.

a We have to walk to school because the car has broken down.

_____ if the car hadn't broken down.

b I won't speak to him because he was so rude to me. I would speak to him _____ .

c I'm not interested in how this mobile works, so I didn't read the manual.

If I'd been interested in how this mobile works, _____ .

d You didn't listen to the instructions so you don't know what to do.

_____ , you'd know what to do.

e I'm annoyed because he borrowed my laptop without asking me first.

_____ if he hadn't borrowed my laptop without asking.

f The sea isn't very warm so we didn't go swimming. _____ we'd have gone swimming.

7 Complete these sentences in an appropriate way. Try to include some mixed conditionals.

a If you show me how to turn on this laptop …

b I'd use the Internet more often if …

c If I'd known you were coming, …

d I might have bought a motorbike if …

e I'd have been amazed if …

Listening

Part 4 Multiple choice

1 Look at the photos of 'cyborgs' and answer a and b.

a Do you know what cyborgs are and what they can do?

b Have you seen any films that feature cyborgs?

2 You are going to listen to a radio programme about Steve Mann, the cyborg in photo 4. First, read questions 1–7, but not the options. Underline the key words in the questions. The first two have been done for you.

1 What do you <u>notice first</u> when you meet Steve Mann?
   A something he's doing
   B something he's wearing
   C something he's looking at

2 <u>Where</u> is the main part of the <u>computer</u>?
   A in the eyepiece
   B at work or at home
   C concealed in his clothing

3 James Fung used the digital eye to
   A fool his friends.
   B entertain his friends.
   C make up a story.

4 What was the problem with the first two versions of the digital eye?
   A They were heavy and uncomfortable.
   B They couldn't be worn.
   C They made him look like a rabbit.

5 Mann and his brother put sensors on the stairs so that
   A they knew when their parents were going to bed.
   B they had time to pretend to be asleep.
   C they could hear what their parents were saying.

6 What makes Mann feel unwell?
   A not wearing the digital eye
   B spending too much time using the digital eye
   C being called a 'cyborg' in the newspapers

7 How does Mann think that wearable computers will affect life in the future?
   A CCTV cameras will become unnecessary.
   B People will become like cyborgs in science-fiction movies.
   C People will have more control over their lives.

3 ◗) Listen and choose the best answer, A, B or C for questions 1–7 in 2.

4 Discuss these questions.

a In what other ways can people be a mixture of 'human' and 'machine'?

b Would you like to wear a computer and eyepiece, like Steve Mann? Why?/Why not?

c Do you agree with Steve Mann that eventually everyone will want to be connected to a computer in this way?

Speaking

Parts 3 and 4

1 Identify the gadgets in the pictures. Do you own any of them? What do you use them for?

2 Make a sentence for each of the gadgets as in the example.

   Example   If we didn't have TV remote controls, we'd have to get up every time we wanted to change channels or adjust the volume.

3 Listen to two students talking about some of the gadgets shown, and answer the following.

   a   Which gadgets do they discuss?

   b   Which gadgets do they decide are the most useful?

   c   Do you agree with their opinions?

4 Listen again and say which of the expressions in the language box they use.

●●● Agreeing

Yes, I agree (with you).
I couldn't agree more.
So do I./Neither do I.
That's right/true.

●●● Disagreeing

I see what you mean, but …
That may be true, but …
Don't you think that … ?
That's a good point, but I …

5 In pairs, do the following, using the phrases in 4 and the **tip** box to help you.

   • Discuss why the gadgets shown are useful, and how life would be different without them.

   • Decide which two gadgets it would be most difficult to live without and why.

> **tip**   You can use these phrases for starting a Part 3 discussion:
> *Let's talk about … first.*
> *We could start by talking about …*
> You can use these phrases for bringing a discussion to a close:
> *I think we need to make a decision.*
> *Shall we try to come an agreement?*

6 Discuss these Part 4 questions.

   a   Do gadgets always make our lives easier?

   b   Can you think of a gadget which is completely unnecessary? Why is it unnecessary?

   c   Do you think we rely too much on computers?

   d   Do computers and gadgets make us antisocial?

Use of English

Part 2 Open cloze

1 Look at these dictionary entries then complete the gaps in sentences a–c.

a Some pressure groups have proposed a ban _____ genetic engineering.

b Who is responsible _____ organising the trip to the science museum?

c Cathy spends a lot of money _____ computer games.

---

ban 0→ /bæn/ *verb, noun*
- *verb* (-nn-) [VN] **1** to decide or say officially that sth is not allowed **SYN** PROHIBIT: *Chemical weapons are banned internationally.* **2** [usually passive] ~ **sb from sth/from doing sth** to order sb not to do sth, go somewhere, etc., especially officially: *He was banned from the meeting.* ◇ *She's been banned from leaving Greece while the allegations are investigated.* ◇ (*BrE*) *He was banned from driving for six months.*
- *noun* ~ (**on sth**) an official rule that says that sth is not allowed: *There is to be a total ban on smoking in the office.* ◇ *to impose/lift a ban*

---

re·spon·sible 0→ /rɪˈspɒnsəbl; NAmE -ˈspɑːn-/ *adj.*
▸ HAVING JOB/DUTY **1** ~ (**for sb/sth**) | ~ (**for doing sth**) having the job or duty of doing sth or taking care of sb/sth, so that you may be blamed if sth goes wrong: *Mike is responsible for designing the entire project.* ◇ *Even where parents no longer live together, they each continue to be responsible for their children.*

---

spend 0→ /spend/ *verb, noun*
- *verb* (spent, spent /spent/) **1** ~ **sth** (**on sth/on doing sth**) to give money to pay for goods, services, etc.: [VN] *I've spent all my money already.* ◇ *She spent £100 on a new dress.* ◇ [VN -ing] *The company has spent thousands of pounds updating their computer systems.* [also V]

Oxford Advanced Learner's Dictionary, 7th edition

2 Complete sentences a–g with these prepositions, then check your answers in a dictionary.

for	on	to	with

a In the future we will rely _____ robots to do menial tasks.

b There's something wrong _____ this DVD player. I can't get it to record.

c Jack Kilby won a Nobel prize in 2000 for his contribution _____ computer science.

d My brother has applied _____ a job with IBM.

e There's a strong demand _____ 3G mobile phones this Christmas.

f Scientists are trying to develop robots that are similar _____ humans.

g You can use this software on a Mac, but it isn't compatible _____ Windows.

3 Read the text opposite, then complete gaps 1–12 with one word each.

4 In which gaps in 3 did you need to add

a a preposition after a verb?

b a preposition after a an adjective?

c a preposition after a noun?

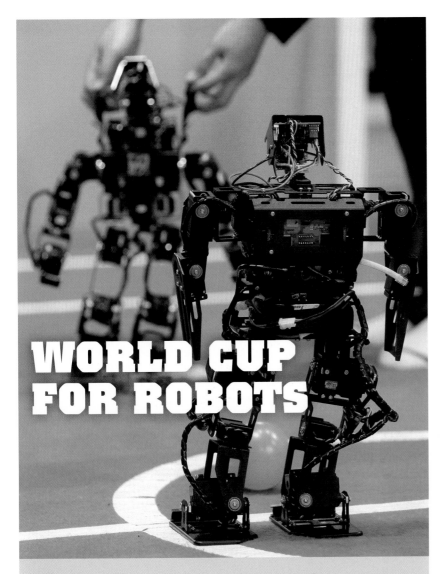

WORLD CUP FOR ROBOTS

This week has seen ^{0} *the* largest ever display of footballing skills – by robots. RoboCup 2007, the World Cup in robotic football, has been taking ^{1}_____ at an American University, with teams ^{2}_____ robots from all around the world participating.

The contestants in the Humanoid League are similar ^{3}_____ children in size, while those competing ^{4}_____ the Nano-Cup are ^{5}_____ small that a microscope is needed to see them. Compared to their human equivalents, robotic footballers ^{6}_____ many advantages: they can keep playing all day, they don't talk back, and ^{7}_____ they ask for more money, you can simply take out their batteries.

Experts are confident that in less ^{8}_____ 50 years' time, football-playing robots capable of taking on ^{9}_____ human side will have ^{10}_____ created. And the technology developed in order ^{11}_____ make RoboCup possible will be used after the World Cup for more important things such ^{12}_____ search and rescue missions.

Vocabulary

Compound nouns

1 Read the compound nouns in the box, then answer questions a and b.

> Internet access   mobile phone
> search engine   artificial intelligence
> instant messaging

a Which of them are formed from two nouns?

b Which of them are formed from an adjective and a noun?

2 Complete a–e with compound nouns from 1.

a *Google* is the most popular _____ on the Internet.

b My teenage daughter sits at her computer all day using _____ to chat with her friends.

c It's illegal to use a _____ while you're driving, unless you have hands-free equipment.

d You can get _____ through any number of Internet service providers.

e Scientists researching _____ have developed computers that can understand human speech.

3 Read the **tip** box, then form compound nouns for a–f using these words. Check your answers and spelling in a dictionary.

> board   lap   text   life
> screen   site

a key_____   d computer_____
b web_____   e _____top
c battery_____   f _____message

tip Some compound nouns are written as a single word, some as two words, and some with a hyphen. Check in your dictionary if you aren't sure.

Writing

Part 1 A letter of complaint

1 Read the letter of complaint opposite and say which of these complaints the customer is making.

a The wrong product was sent.

b They were overcharged.

c The product was damaged.

d The product was delivered late.

e The product didn't work.

f They didn't get a response to their complaints.

2 Read the phrases in the language box and say which ones Sheila uses in her letter.

●●● Expressing contrast

| Despite (the fact that) … |
| In spite of (the fact that) … |
| Although/Even though … |
| However, … |
| … whereas … |
| … but … |

Dear Sir or Madam,

Order number RX5468J

I am writing to complain about a Sonitech LCD television which I bought recently from your website, www.tvsanddvdsgalore.co.uk. Although you claim your service is 'unbeatable', it certainly leaves a lot to be desired.

First of all, I ordered a 32-inch television, but you sent me one with a 28-inch screen. Secondly, I placed the order on 17th December, but despite the fact that you guaranteed to deliver it before Christmas, it didn't arrive until 28th December. This was extremely disappointing as it was a Christmas present for my husband.

Finally, I should like to complain about your customer service department. I contacted you on a number of occasions via your website. However, I did not receive a reply to my emails or even an acknowledgement that you had received them. I also tried phoning, but the line was either engaged or I was put through to an answering machine.

I would be most grateful if you would arrange to collect the television and give me a full refund. I look forward to hearing from you.

Yours faithfully

Sheila Watson

3 Complete sentences a–f with an appropriate phrase from 2.

a .... not receiving the goods, my credit card was charged the full amount.

b The handset I have received is purple, ... the one in the advertisement is blue.

c .... I ordered the computer in May, it did not arrive until August.

d The special offer included free headphones. ...., these did not arrive.

e The technical support staff were friendly .... not very knowledgeable.

f I have heard nothing from the manufacturers, ... having written to them twice.

4 Read the task below, and the advertisement with the notes. For each note write a sentence using one of the phrases in 2. In one clause mention what you expected or what the website claimed, in the other clause say what actually happened.

Example Although you promised to deliver the phone before Christmas, I didn't receive it until 27th December.

You saw this advertisement on the Internet and ordered a mobile phone. You were not happy with the service you received. Read the advertisement and the notes you made. Write a letter of complaint to the company, mentioning the things you were unhappy about. Ask for a full refund of your money.

5 Write a letter of 120–150 words. Include the sentences you wrote in 4.

Didn't work.

Saw it cheaper.

Delivered late.

Wrong model.
Sent Mobifone 1100.

Overcharged me.

CHEAP MOBILES!

Reliable mobiles at unbeatable prices!
Find your mobile cheaper on another website
and we'll refund the difference.

Order now for delivery before Christmas.

Mobifone 612
More info
ONLY £100
Add to basket

Voicetech V220
More info
ONLY £100
Add to basket

Mitsuda D600
More info
ONLY £110
Add to basket

FREE DELIVERY!

About us   Contact   Terms and conditions   FAQs   Privacy policy   Site map

Review

1 Read the definitions in a–d and complete the words they define.

a something that helps you use your mobile phone without having to hold it to your ear
  w_____ headset

b a way of sending very quick text messages between computers
  i_____ m_____

c to send a written message between mobile phones
  t_____

d the sound a mobile phone makes when someone is calling you
  r_____

2 Make complete sentences by matching a–h with 1–8.

a More and more people are getting interested
b The high demand
c I am responsible
d You can't rely
e There's a total ban
f My sister has applied
g George seems to be completely unable to learn
h The huge increase in air travel has made a significant contribution

1 on Mark to keep a secret.
2 for a place to study medicine at university.
3 to global warming.
4 from his mistakes.
5 in technology.
6 for oil has pushed prices up.
7 on smoking in our office.
8 for keeping the website updated.

3 Complete sentences a–e with compound nouns. One part of each compound (either the first or the second) is given in brackets.

a I've got a wireless _____ on my computer. (key)

b If you leave your MP3 player switched on, you may shorten its _____ . (life)

c _____ is an area of computer science that focuses on creating machines that can think. (intelligence)

d My dad takes his _____ with him every morning so that he can work on the train. (lap)

e If you're planning to sell goods on the Internet, you need a well-designed _____ . (web)

4 Complete the sentences with a word or phrase that expresses contrast. There may be more than one possible answer.

a _____ he's very wealthy, he's very careful with his money.

b iPods are fantastic gadgets. They are, _____ , quite a bit more expensive than most MP3 players.

c John doesn't have a mobile phone, _____ his sister Kate has three!

d I do like Peter, _____ I have to say, he can be very moody and difficult.

e Scientists have built computers that can understand speech. _____ this, I don't think they will ever develop a machine that can actually think.

f I thought I'd lost my mobile. _____ , it turned up in my wife's handbag.

5 Correct the mistakes in these sentences.

a I'm writing to complain of a DVD player I bought from you.

b You have charged me over by £10.

c I tried to contact to you on a number of occasions, without success.

d I would be most grateful when you would give me a full refund.

e I look forward to hear from you.

Make a difference ¹²

Lead in

1 Imagine that your favourite leisure centre is about to be closed down and you want to save it. Read the ideas below and say which action is most likely to have an impact, in your opinion.

  a writing to a local politician

  b starting an Internet petition

  c organising a protest march

  d handing out leaflets in the street

  e putting up posters around town

  f contacting the local press/radio/TV

  g staging a publicity stunt (e.g. chaining yourselves to the gates)

  h painting slogans on walls around town

2 Have you ever taken part in any of the actions from 1 or do you know someone who has? If so, did they have any effect?

3 Discuss what you think these charities and organisations aim to do and how. Try to agree on the three most important and effective.

 Save the Children

GREENPEACE

 WWF

 Oxfam

Reading

Part 3 Multiple matching

1 Read the text opposite quickly, then match sections A–D with the photos.

2 Read the text again carefully, then for questions 1–15, choose from the people or groups A–D.

Which person or group

1 risked death or serious injury
2 targets people who take themselves too seriously?
3 protested against a company's methods of food production?
4 has very well-known supporters?
5 made a long journey on their hands and knees?
6 ate an unusual meal as a way of protesting?
7 is more likely to repeat the stunt if people get annoyed?
8 was very unpopular with animal rights groups?
9 acted in support of peace?
10 got into trouble with the law?
11 used an unusual costume to gain media attention?
12 uses food as a weapon?
13 found a protest very unpleasant?
14 has performed similar stunts in various countries?
15 makes well-known people the object of his stunts?

3 Complete the verb + noun collocations in a–g then check your answers by finding them in the text.

| bring | cause | earn | become | make | raise | have |

a to .... front page news (l. 4)
b to .... a dislike for somebody (l. 15)
c to .... a target (l. 31)
d to .... (public) awareness (l. 40)
e to .... something to someone's attention (l. 46)
f to .... a scandal (l. 61)
g to .... yourself a nickname (l. 86)

4 Giving reasons, say which of the stunts described was, in your opinion

a the most unusual
b the most physically demanding
c for the best cause.

PERFORMING PROTESTS

WHEN a group of American protestors threw 40,000 kilos of tea into Boston Harbour in 1773 as part of their campaign against unfair taxes, they made front page news around the world. More than a century and a half later, one of the best-known protestors in history, Mahatma Gandhi, talked about being inspired by the 'famous Boston Tea Party'. Why was it so significant? Not because it was particularly successful in political terms, but because it demonstrated the power of the publicity stunt. In today's society of 24-hour news coverage, a good stunt is an even more valuable weapon for campaigners – and the more attention-grabbing it is, the better.

1

A Noël Godin

15 Noël Godin is a Belgian writer, critic and actor, who has
a particular dislike for public figures whom he considers
to be self-important or lacking in a sense of humour. His
form of protest against these people is novel: he pushes
a large cream pie into their face. His most famous
20 victim is probably Bill Gates, head of software company
Microsoft and one of the wealthiest men in the world.
He 'cream-pied' Gates in 1998, an incident which made
it onto news bulletins all around the world. He has also
singled out several French celebrities, including politician
25 Nicolas Sarkozy and film-maker Jean-Luc Godard. Godin
insists that his actions are non-violent; he is careful to
use very soft cakes filled with cream and perhaps a little
chocolate. If his victim reacts badly to the stunt, Godin
does it again at a later date. The French philosopher
30 Bernard-Henri Lévy became so angry with Godin that he
has become a regular target, and has now been cream-
pied five times.

B PETA

PETA (People for the Ethical Treatment of Animals)
claims to be the largest animal rights organisation in the
35 world. It has several high-profile faces behind it, including
Hollywood star Pamela Anderson, who help to focus media
attention on their campaigns. One ongoing campaign is
against the fast food chain KFC, whom they accuse of
animal cruelty, a charge the company denies. In 2005, to
40 raise public awareness of this campaign, a PETA volunteer
in the USA dressed up as a giant chicken and, sitting in
a wheelchair, repeatedly crossed the road outside a KFC
franchise in Columbia, South Carolina. Customers who
visited the restaurant during this time were not dissuaded
45 from buying food there, but the protest achieved its wider
objective: it appeared on TV news, thus bringing the issue
to the attention of the public.

C Mark McGowan

Mark McGowan is part protestor, part performance artist.
His eye-catching stunts are intended to attract attention
50 and make people think. In 2003, in order to protest
about students having to borrow money to pay for their
university studies, he used his nose to push a peanut
along the pavement for 10 kilometres, finishing outside
the Prime Minister's official residence in Downing Street.
55 In December 2005, he crawled from London to Canterbury
(approximately 130 kilometres) to raise awareness of
loneliness at Christmas. Earlier that year, he turned on
a tap in an art gallery in London and planned to leave
it running for a year, wasting 15 million litres of water
60 – although the water company he was protesting against
forced him to turn it off after a month. In 2007, he caused
a scandal by eating a swan as a protest against the
monarchy. According to an old law, all swans in the UK
are the property of the queen, and eating one is a crime.
65 However, it was not the police who objected but animal
rights activists! Eating the swan was not an enjoyable
experience, especially as McGowan is a long-standing
vegetarian. 'I suffer for my art,' he said. 'It was disgusting,
greasy and fatty.'

D Alain Robert

70 In March 2003, Alain Robert climbed one of the tallest
buildings in Paris, the 180m TotalFinaElf skyscraper,
with his bare hands. A crowd of onlookers and officials
watched nervously as he made the ascent without ropes
or any other form of safety equipment, wearing a T-shirt
75 bearing an anti-war slogan. The crowd cheered when, after
45 minutes, he safely reached the top of the building,
where the police were waiting to arrest him. Climbing tall
buildings, with or without permission from the authorities,
has become something of an obsession for Robert. He
80 claims it began at the age of 12 when he forgot his keys
and was locked out of his parents' eighth-floor apartment.
Instead of waiting until they returned home, Alain climbed
up the outside of the tower block and got in through a
window. Since then, he has climbed some of the tallest
85 buildings in the world, including the Petronas Twin Towers
in Malaysia – twice. No wonder he has earned himself the
nickname 'the French Spiderman'.

Vocabulary

Achievement and success

1 Complete phrases a–e with the words below.

> achieve   ambition   manage   succeed   target

a fulfil/realise a/an _____

b reach a/an _____

c _____ success

d _____ to do something

e _____ in doing something

2 Rewrite sentences a–d using the verb in brackets in the correct form.

a The protestors were not successful in changing the government's policy. (manage)

b Sophia Coppola was successful in the film industry at a young age. (achieve)

c Despite winning *Pop Idol*, she was unable to make a career in music. (succeed)

d Last year, students from our school cycled around Britain to raise money for Oxfam, and successfully raised a figure of £60,000. (reach)

3 Complete sentences a–e with the words below.

> achievable   achievement   realisation
> success   successful

a Winning an Olympic gold medal was the _____ of a lifelong ambition.

b Failure is not an option; we expect _____ .

c The first _____ non-stop flight across the Atlantic was made in 1919.

d Discovering the tomb of Tutankhamen was Howard Carter's greatest _____ .

e Learning to drive in a month is difficult, but _____ .

4 In pairs, tell each other about

- an ambition that you have realised.
- an ambition that you have not yet fulfilled.
- something that you hope to achieve within the next year.

Grammar

Causative verbs: *have, make, let* and *get* GR p175

1 Complete gaps 1–5 in the text with the correct forms of *have*, *let*, *get* or *make*.

Students back hair protest

Students at a college have staged a protest at the treatment of a fellow student. The row began when Gavin Trent, 17, [1]_____ his hair dyed with the colours of his favourite football team. At first, the school would not [2]_____ Gavin attend classes with his new hairstyle, claiming that it might [3]_____ fans of other teams become aggressive. After discussions, Gavin [4]_____ the school to change its mind and allow him back into school, but he was [5]_____ to wear a hat during lessons.

2 Complete sentences a–g with the verbs in the box. Use the correct form of *have* + part participle.

> cut   decorate   deliver   develop
> service   steal   take

a I must _____ my car _____ . The engine's making an odd sound.

b We _____ our living-room _____ last week. It looks fantastic with its fresh coat of paint.

c Many celebrities hate _____ their photos _____ by press photographers.

d When did you last _____ your hair _____ ?

e We _____ three newspapers _____ on Sundays.

f One advantage of a digital camera is that you don't need to _____ the pictures _____ .

g If you leave your mobile phone visible in the car you're likely to _____ it _____ .

3 Look at the pictures and say what work the owners of this house have had done. Write sentences as in the example using the verbs below.

build	cut	paint	remove
repair	replace		

Example   They've had the front door replaced.

4 Complete sentences a–f using *make*, in active or passive form, and an appropriate verb.

a The film had a very sad ending that .... me ....

b When I was younger I .... 10 minutes of violin practice every evening by my parents.

c In the nineteenth century many British children .... long hours in factories.

d I think I've made myself clear. Don't .... me .... myself.

e That song always .... me .... of college. I used to listen to it all the time as a student.

f At the surgery Sam .... for over an hour to see the doctor.

5 In pairs, talk about what your parents made you do or let you do when you were younger, as in the example. Use the phrases below and your own ideas.

- stay up late
- tidy your bedroom
- learn a musical instrument
- wash your own clothes
- surf the Internet
- have a computer in your bedroom
- watch anything you liked on TV

Example   Did your parents let you stay up late?

Not very late. I had to go to bed before seven until I was about 10 years old.

Did they make you tidy your bedroom?

Yes, they did, but not very often.

6 Say what would you do in each of these situations using *have*, *get*, *make* and *let*.

a You are at a party and somebody spills orange juice on your new jacket.

b Your best friend asks you to lend them a lot of money.

c You see a group of teenagers in the street painting graffiti on a wall.

d You have ordered some books on the Internet but they haven't arrived two weeks later.

e Your neighbours' son keeps on kicking his ball into your garden.

f You see a young woman shoplifting.

Listening

Part 2 Sentence completion

1 Look at the photos. See if you can name the celebrities and match them with the campaigns that they have supported.

a make poverty history
b fair trade
c ban the fur trade
d campaign to protect native people

2 •)) Listen to the extract from a radio programme and check your ideas in 1.

3 •)) Listen again and complete sentences 1–10.

1 Recently a lot of celebrities have become . involved in ....

2 The pop star Sting started working for charities during the ....

3 Mike says that the purpose of Sting's foundation is to protect the .... and its inhabitants.

4 Sting and the Kayapo leader travelled the world for .... months.

5 Lisa belongs to the *Coldplay* ....

6 *Coldplay* give away .... of the money the band makes to charity.

7 *Coldplay* performed at a charity concert in ....

8 The British singer Jamelia agreed to be covered in .... feathers.

9 Jamelia said that to many fans .... are less important than musicians.

10 Naomi Campbell was booed at a fashion show because she wore a ....

4 Can you name any other celebrities who are associated with charities? Why do you think celebrities get involved in charity work?

Speaking

Part 2

1 Match these words and phrases to photos 1 and 2.

> enclosure   freedom   man-made
> natural habitat   protected
> social group   solitary

> **tip** Begin by making factual statements about the photos, including the most obvious similarities and differences. Then move on to comments which involve opinion or speculation.

2 Read the **tip** box, then decide which of a–g are factual, and which convey an opinion or speculation.

   a Photo 1 shows a solitary lion whereas photo 2 shows a group of lions.

   b I would imagine that the lion in photo 1 is quite bored.

   c The lion in photo 1 is in a zoo or safari park.

   d The lion in photo 1 probably has to cope with crowds of noisy visitors every day.

   e It's likely that the lions in photo 2 are more exposed to dangers.

   f The lion in photo 1 looks slightly depressed, in my view.

   g Photo 2 shows a group of lions in their natural environment.

3 Compare the photos and say how life is different for the lions, following the advice in the **tip** box.

4 In pairs, decide which lions have the better life, in your opinion, and why.

5 Say whether you agree or disagree with these statements. Give reasons.

   a It's cruel to keep animals in zoos.

   b Zoos help to save animals from extinction.

   c It doesn't matter if animal species become extinct. It's natural.

Use of English

Part 1 Multiple-choice cloze

1 Find the adjectives in italics in a–h in a dictionary and say whether one or both are possible in the sentences.

   a Most of the information in that article is *false/untrue*.

   b In the past, most people over the age of 50 had *false/untrue* teeth.

   c The campsite is next to a *broad/wide* river.

   d This leaflet will give you a *broad/wide* idea of the services we offer.

   e He refused to discuss his divorce, saying it was a *personal/private* matter.

   f Stories are usually more convincing when they're written from *personal/private* experience.

   g The Chrysler Building is one of the *highest/tallest* buildings in New York.

   h He poured the lemonade into a *high/tall* glass.

2 Read the text opposite, ignoring the gaps, and say whether sentences a–c about Daryl Hannah are true or false.

   a She wants people to try 'green living' and thinks they will like it.

   b She rarely talks about environmental issues because she dislikes confrontation.

   c She makes videos about environmental issues but is not committed to them in her personal life.

3 Read the text again carefully and for 1–12 decide which answer (A, B, C or D) best fits each gap.

0	A arrives	(B) pulls	C reaches	D stops
1	A tall	B high	C extended	D lengthy
2	A single	B moment	C moment's	D second
3	A scene	B picture	C view	D animation
4	A private	B personal	C personable	D separate
5	A contained	B followed	C added	D included
6	A bang	B crash	C splash	D smash
7	A for	B of	C to	D in
8	A making	B bringing	C having	D letting
9	A possible	B available	C ready	D easy
10	A do	B have	C give	D make
11	A more	B many	C far	D much
12	A up	B down	C back	D out

Green living

A black Chevrolet ⁰............ into a filling station and out steps Hollywood star Daryl Hannah. She undoes the petrol cap and starts filling up. Then she pours herself a ¹............ glass of the green fuel, straight from the pump, and drinks it without a ²............ hesitation.

This attention-grabbing ³............ appears on Hannah's 'vlog' (video blog) and is part of her new identity. The vlog, which features a new segment every week, reveals Hannah's ⁴............ experience of the latest in green living. Topics have ⁵............ environmentally friendly buildings, vegan diet, gorillas in Rwanda and biodiesel – one of Hannah's favourite issues.

Best known for her roles in ⁶............ hits like *Blade Runner*, *Splash* and *Kill Bill*, Hannah has a long-standing commitment ⁷............ environmental living. But she's only recently started ⁸............ her green lifestyle to the attention of the public.

'People have to know that there are options ⁹............ to us today,' she said. 'There is another way, and it is practical and applicable now.'

Hannah's focus on solutions reaches people in a way that protest and confrontation can't. All she wants is for people to ¹⁰............ it a try.

'If you eat only vegetables and fruits that you grow yourself in your garden, or organic food,' she says, 'it tastes so ¹¹............ better and is better for you, you can't really go ¹²............ to supermarket food.'

Vocabulary

Compound adjectives

1 Match a–h with 1–8 to form compound adjectives.

a	eye-	1	quenching
b	labour-	2	catching
c	thirst-	3	saving
d	record-	4	warming
e	time-	5	watering
f	heart	6	consuming
g	mouth-	7	eating
h	meat-	8	breaking

2 Complete sentences a–h with compound adjectives from 1.

a Tyrannosaurus Rex was a .... dinosaur whereas most dinosaurs were herbivores and ate plants.

b .... devices like washing machines and dishwashers have made life much easier.

c I don't think people will notice such a small advertisement – we need something more
....

d Fizzy drinks aren't as .... as water.

e She ran the last lap of the race in just 45 seconds – a .... achievement.

f Picking grapes by hand is very .... so the job is done by machines in many vineyards.

g There was a .... story on the news last night about a teenager who dived into a river and pulled a little girl to safety.

h This book contain hundreds of .... recipes. I highly recommend it.

3 Rewrite sentences a–e replacing the underlined phrases with compound adjectives, as in the example.

Example   He used to be a layabout, <u>who ate chocolate and</u> <u>watched TV</u>.

He used to be a chocolate-eating, TV-watching layabout.

a Newspapers always put headlines <u>that will grab people's attention</u> on the front page.

b He's always coming up with interesting ideas <u>to make money</u>.

c My uncle runs a company <u>that cleans windows</u>.

d In Nicaragua, Jinotega and Matagalpa are the largest areas <u>where they grow coffee</u>.

e The film <u>which won an award</u> is being shown on TV tonight

Writing

Part 2 An article

1 Read the exam task below, then number the paragraphs in the article in the correct order. Say which words helped you.

2 Say which of 1–9 are
   a usually used in formal writing
   b usually used in informal writing
   c used in both formal and informal writing

   1 not only … but also
   2 furthermore
   3 in addition
   4 on top of that
   5 what's more
   6 to make matters worse
   7 moreover
   8 as well as
   9 besides

3 Find five of the phrases in 2 in the article.

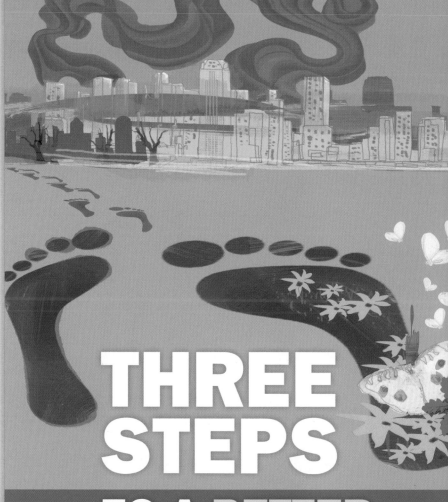

THREE STEPS
TO A BETTER ENVIRONMENT

How could the environment be improved in your town or village? Tell us your ideas for three changes that you think should be made.

We will publish the most interesting articles next month.

☐ First, I would have the multi-storey car park in the town centre demolished. Not only is it a very ugly building, but it also attracts criminals, especially after dark. Moreover, removing the car park would make people use public transport for coming into town.

☐ To sum up, if you visited Monkton, I'm sure you'd agree that these simple changes would make it a much more attractive town, as well as improving the quality of life of its inhabitants.

☐ Thirdly, I would ban lorries from driving through the town centre. They cause a lot of noise and pollution and what's more, they put people off cycling, because cyclists are afraid they will get knocked off their bikes.

☐ We would all like to make our towns and villages more pleasant places to live and work in. If I could make three changes to my hometown of Monkton, this is what I would do.

☐ Secondly, I would have the area around the lake cleaned up. At the moment, the banks are covered with litter. In addition, I would get the council to install some litter bins and erect some picnic tables.

4 Correct the underlined mistakes in a–e.

   a Besides <u>to ban</u> cars from the centre, I'd have the roads resurfaced.

   b Cars cause a lot of pollution as well as <u>they are</u> noisy.

   c Not only <u>there are</u> not enough buses but they are old and dirty.

   d <u>Moreover</u> is the town hall old, it's also ugly.

   e In addition to <u>clean up</u> the park I'd have a children's playground installed.

5 Read the **tip** box, then find examples of how the writer has attempted to involve the reader.

> **tip** Involve your readers by addressing them directly, and by using the personal pronouns *I, we* and *you.*

6 Imagine you have seen the announcement in 1 in a magazine called *Green Issues*. Work in pairs and decide on three areas for change, using the ideas below to help you.

> air quality   noise   recycling
> public transport   buildings and roads
> facilities   shops   parks and public
> spaces   trees and plants

7 For each of the areas you chose in 6, write two sentences about how things could be improved. Try to use each of these grammatical structures at least once.

   a have something done

   b get someone to do something

   c make something + adjective

   d make someone do something

   e would/wouldn't let someone do something

   Example I'd make people pick up their litter, or pay a fine.

8 Write your answer to the task in 1 in 120–180 words.

Review

1 Complete a–d using these verbs in the correct form.

> manage   reach   realise   succeed

a The online petition _____ in forcing the government to change their policy.

b My grandfather always wanted to own a small hotel. He was nearly 60 years old before he _____ his ambition.

c Protestors _____ to throw paint over the visiting politician.

d Local shops hope to raise $1 million for Africa, and so far they are about halfway to _____ their target.

2 Complete the sentences using a word formed from the word in brackets.

Example   The exam was difficult, but I found it _____ (manage)

The exam was difficult, but I found it manageable.

a The invention of dynamite was Alfred Nobel's best-known _____ . (achieve)

b All across Europe we must _____ reduce carbon emissions. (success)

c Meeting President Clinton was the _____ of a longstanding ambition. (realise)

d Fair trade is only _____ with the cooperation of richer nations. (achieve)

e After several _____ attempts to find work, Kevin moved to a different town. (success)

3 Rewrite sentences a–e replacing the compound adjectives with a clause.

Example   It was a life-changing experience for me.

It was an experience that changed my life.

a There are three Chinese-speaking members of staff where I work.

b I've just bought a bread-making machine.

c A tarantula is a large, bird-eating spider.

d This magazine is full of money-saving ideas.

e The goalkeeper was not really injured – it was just a time-wasting tactic.

4 Read the text below and decide which answer (A, B, C or D) best fits each gap 1–10.

1 A biggest   B strongest   C largest   D grandest
2 A reply   B response   C answer   D solution
3 A engineered   B filled   C fed   D powered
4 A any   B many   C much   D some
5 A increased   B raised   C grew   D lifted
6 A difference   B change   C alteration   D warming
7 A classes   B subjects   C lectures   D lessons
8 A absolute   B whole   C complete   D total
9 A does   B deals   C makes   D runs
10 A do   B get   C have   D make

BIG GREEN GATHERING

One of the (1) _____ questions in the battle against climate change is: can our modern lifestyle really be sustained by alternative energy sources alone? A community called The Big Green Gathering is attempting to prove that the (2) _____ to this question is yes. Even though the community has a population of 20,000 people, it uses no fossil fuels at all. Vehicles within the community are (3) _____ by vegetable oil or grass. Solar and wind power provide the electricity for the (4) _____ nightclubs and bars.

The Big Green Gathering (5) _____ out of the hippy movement of the 1970s, which promoted an alternative lifestyle. But these days, you don't have to be a hippy to care deeply about climate (6) _____ . It's something we all should worry about, and festivals like these can teach us important (7) _____ about how to make our lifestyle more ecologically friendly.

In some ways, this is like any other music festival, with a main stage, giant loudspeakers and rows of lights. Watching and listening as a band performs on stage, you would assume that that enormous petrol-driven generators were being used to provide power. But in fact, the (8) _____ thing is powered by solar panels. And away from the music, you can meet Alex Gadsen, who (9) _____ the festival laundrette. Alex has invented a pedal-powered washing machine, so you can get a work-out as you (10) _____ your washing!

Appendix

1 The circle of life

Lead in page 9

3 Paris Hilton (photo 1) and Nikki Hilton (photo 6) are sisters.

Sophia Coppola (photo 2) and Nicolas Cage (photo 4) are cousins.

Jade Jagger (photo 3) are Mick Jagger (photo 7) are daughter and father.

Joaquin Phoenix (photo 5) and River Phoenix (photo 8) were brothers.

10 All in the mind

Lead in page 117

3

What's your **learning style**?

Mostly 'A' answers: You have a visual learning style. You learn best by looking at pictures, charts, films and diagrams. You remember from seeing rather than listening.

Mostly 'B' answers: You have an auditory learning style. You learn best by listening to explanations, talking, and repeating things out loud. Your remember things you have heard more than things you have seen.

Mostly 'C' answers: You have a kinaesthetic learning style. You learn best by doing, moving and touching. The best way for you to learn a language, for example, is by interacting with other learners.

10

Lead in page 117

4 Look at the photos and answer these questions.

  a Which person didn't introduce themselves earlier?

  b Can you remember the other five names?

  c What else can you remember about them?

  d Did anybody in the class remember everything about each person?

Grammar page 121

5 1 A 2 C 3 B 4 A 5 A 6 C

11 Man and machine

Lead in page 129

2

ARE YOU A TECHNOPHILE OR TECHNOPHOBE?

Add up your points: a = 3, b = 2, c = 1. Then check what your score means.

14–18 You are a technophile. You are interested in gadgets and comfortable with innovations and new technology.

8–13 You aren't very interested in technology for its own sake, but in what technology can do for you.

6–8 You are a technophobe. You aren't interested in how things work. You dislike, and perhaps are afraid of, new technology.

Writing Guide

Part 1 A letter or email

You saw this job advertisement in a magazine called *Jobs Abroad*. Read the advertisement and the notes you have made. Then write an email application for the job, using all your notes. Write 120–150 words.

CAMP UK

We are looking for Sports and Activities Organisers to work in our summer camp for teenagers in Scotland.

Email us and tell us why you want the job and what you could bring to it. — *tell them*

It doesn't matter where you come from as long as you have a good command of English. — *give details.*

Accommodation will be provided. — *ask for details. is it free?*

We will be interviewing short-listed applicants in London. — *ask when*

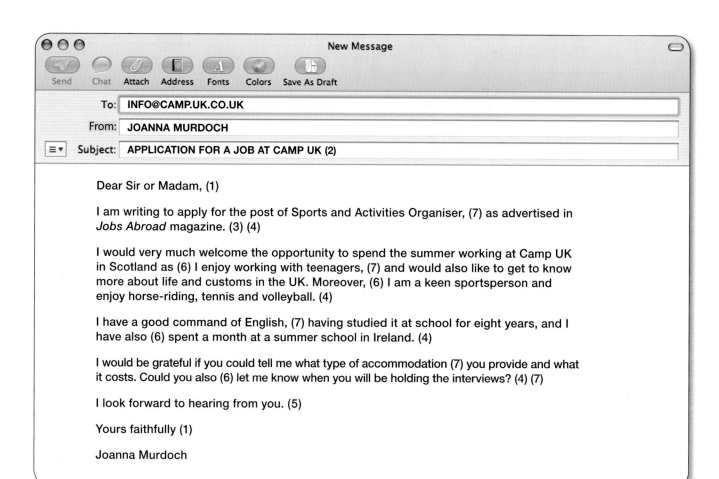

New Message

Send Chat Attach Address Fonts Colors Save As Draft

To: INFO@CAMP.UK.CO.UK

From: JOANNA MURDOCH

Subject: APPLICATION FOR A JOB AT CAMP UK (2)

Dear Sir or Madam, (1)

I am writing to apply for the post of Sports and Activities Organiser, (7) as advertised in *Jobs Abroad* magazine. (3) (4)

I would very much welcome the opportunity to spend the summer working at Camp UK in Scotland as (6) I enjoy working with teenagers, (7) and would also like to get to know more about life and customs in the UK. Moreover, (6) I am a keen sportsperson and enjoy horse-riding, tennis and volleyball. (4)

I have a good command of English, (7) having studied it at school for eight years, and I have also (6) spent a month at a summer school in Ireland. (4)

I would be grateful if you could tell me what type of accommodation (7) you provide and what it costs. Could you also (6) let me know when you will be holding the interviews? (4) (7)

I look forward to hearing from you. (5)

Yours faithfully (1)

Joanna Murdoch

1 If you begin the letter or email with *Dear Sir or Madam*, finish with *Yours faithfully*. If you begin with *Dear (Mr Smith)*, finish with *Yours sincerely*.

2 If you are asked to write an email, you will be given a printed email heading so you do not need to make one up.

3 Start by saying why you are writing.

4 Divide the letter into three or four short paragraphs, each with its own topic.

5 If you expect a reply to your letter write 'I look forward to hearing from you.' after the final paragraph.

6 Use linking words to join ideas and sentences.

7 Refer to the input information but do not copy out large parts of it.

8 Use a style appropriate to the situation, and maintain the same style throughout the letter or email.

●●● **Phrase Bank**

Giving a reason for writing

I am writing to apply for …

I am writing to enquire about …

I am writing to complain about …

I am writing in response to …

Applying for a job

I have considerable experience of …

I consider myself to be …

I would welcome the opportunity to …

Requesting information

I'd be grateful if you could tell me …

Could you please let me know … ?

Complaining

I wish to complain in the strongest possible terms about …

I am not satisfied with …

Part 2 A letter

You have received a letter from a friend in an English-speaking country, telling you what they did in the summer holidays. Write a letter back telling them what you did in the holidays. Write 120–180 words.

1 Invent a name for the person you are writing to.

2 Mention the correspondence that you have received. Thank the person for it or react to it in some way.

3 Use informal language, contractions, some short sentences, phrasal verbs and (one or two) exclamation marks.

4 Divide the letter into three or four short paragraphs, each with its own topic.

5 Finish the letter with an informal phrase such as *Love, Lots of love, Take care* or *All the best*.

Dear Sally (1)

Thanks for your letter. (2) It sounds like you had a great summer. I really enjoyed the holidays too, but they weren't long enough! (3) (4)

As soon as school broke up I went off to Spain with my parents. We stayed in a lovely little village on the north coast and spent loads of time on the beach or walking in the mountains. (4)

When I came back (3) I spent three works working in a café. At first I was in the kitchen, washing up – I hated that. But after a while the boss let me take orders and serve customers. That was much more fun, and I got some good tips too. In the final week of the holiday I went and stayed with my cousins. We just lazed around and spent most of the time watching DVDs. Then it was back to school. (4)

Anyway I'd (3) better stop here as I've got quite a lot of homework to get through before tomorrow. (4)

How's school going? Write again soon with more news.

Love (5)

Laura

●●● Phrase Bank

Starting the letter
Thanks very much for your letter. It was good to hear from you.
How have you been?
How are things with you and your family?
I'm sorry I haven't written for ages. I've been …

Finishing the letter
Anyway, that's all for now.
I'd better stop here. I've got to …
Give my love/regards to …
Write again soon.
I look forward to seeing you again soon.

Part 2 A review

You recently saw this notice in a magazine.

BOOK REVIEWS

Have you read any books recently? If so, please write and tell us about one of them. Say what you liked or didn't like about the story and the characters.

Write a review of 120–180 words.

I **recently read** *The Phantom of the Opera*, a novel written in 1910 by Gaston Leroux. It has been adapted a number of times for the cinema and also made into an immensely successful musical. (1) (4)

It's set in Paris and is the story of Erik (the 'phantom'), a menacing figure who lives hidden away in the basement of the opera house. He is in love with Christine, an opera singer, but she in turn loves a young aristocrat called Raoul. (3) The plot is very intricate with lots of twists and turns, which keep the reader turning the pages. (2) (4)

My main criticism of the book is the characterisation. (2) The characters are unmemorable and rather shallow. It is often difficult to understand why they do certain things, for example, (6) when Christine chooses to have a conversation with Raoul on the roof of the opera house. (4)

To sum up, I enjoyed this 'gothic' horror story despite the weaknesses in the characterisation. However, I'd only recommend it to people who really enjoy horror or ghost stories. (4) (5)

1 In the first paragraph say what you are reviewing and give relevant key information (such as the author of a book or the director of a film).

2 You can give both positive and negative opinions.

3 Say briefly what happens in the book, play, film, etc.

4 Put each topic in a separate paragraph.

5 Summarise your opinion in the final paragraph and give a recommendation (either positive or negative)

6 If you can, give examples from the story to support your opinions, but make sure you keep within the word limit.

●●● Phrase Bank

Giving background information
I recently read/saw …
One of my favourite films/books is …

Describing a story
It's set in …
It tells the story of …
There's a twist at the end.
The main character is …

Giving a recommendation
I can thoroughly recommend this book/film.
Go and see this film/read this book. You won't be disappointed.
I certainly wouldn't recommend this film/play.
Don't bother reading …/going to see … . It isn't worth it.

Part 2 An article

You have seen this announcement in a magazine.

We are offering a prize for the best article with the title:

A town that I really like.

Write an article of 120–180 words.

A town that I really like

Have you ever visited the south west of England? (1) I was brought up there, in a town called Kingsbury, and in my opinion you couldn't choose a better place to live or just to visit. (3)

Kingsbury is only a couple miles from the coast, where you can find lots of fantastic beaches. The surrounding countryside is very beautiful and there are some wild, woodland areas nearby, ideal for walking and other outdoor activities. (3)

The town itself is very pretty, with narrow winding streets and lots of interesting old buildings. There are quite a few good cafés and restaurants and the shops are excellent. Every weekend there's a farmers' market when you can fresh local meat and vegetables. (3)

Finally, the pace of life is slower than in the city. People are friendly and aren't always in a hurry. They have more time to stop and chat with you. (3)

So, whatever you're looking for in a small town – attractive buildings, great shops, nice places to eat and drink, good leisure facilities – Kingsbury has them all. (3) (4)

1 Involve the reader. You can address them directly, especially with questions.

2 Use an informal, lively style. Avoid using a lot of formal language.

3 Divide the information into clearly organised paragraphs.

4 Finish by summarising what you have said, and giving your opinion, if appropriate.

●●● Phrase Bank

Involving the reader
Have you ever … ?
What would you do/think if … ?
Can you imagine … ?
You might think that … , but …

Giving opinions
In my opinion/view, …
I think/believe that …
As far as I'm concerned, …
To my mind, …
Personally, I find/think …

Part 2 A report

The college where you study wants to raise some money to buy new books and DVDs for the library. The principal has asked you to write report recommending the best way to raise the money.

Write a report of 120–180 words.

> **The purpose of this report is to consider different ways of raising money to pay for new books and DVDs for the school library, and to recommend the best course of action.** (1)
>
> ## Prize draw (2)
>
> One idea is (5) to sell numbered tickets and offer prizes. Students and teachers could be asked (5) to bring in unwanted items that would be suitable as prizes, and the school could also approach (5) local shops and restaurants who might be willing to contribute prizes.
>
> ## Sponsored run (2)
>
> Another possibility would be (5) to organise a sponsored run around the local park. Students could ask their friends and family to give a certain amount for every mile they complete.
>
> ## My recommendation (2)
>
> I recommend that we organise a sponsored run. Although the advantage of offering prizes is that it would be easier to organise, the plan might come to nothing (5) if we are unable to find enough suitable prizes or sell enough tickets. A sponsored run, on the other hand, is likely to raise more money and would have the added benefit of involving more of the students and staff. (6)

1 Start with an introduction setting out the aim of the report.

2 Organise the information into sections. Use headings if appropriate.

3 You can use numbered or bullet points.

4 Use fairly formal language.

5 Express opinions impersonally.

6 Finish with a conclusion giving your recommendation.

●●● Phrase Bank

Expressing your opinions
The aim/purpose of this report is to …

Discussing pros and cons
One advantage/disadvantage of … is …
There are strong arguments in favour of/against …

Making additional points
I recommend that …
It would be advisable to …
It would be a good idea to/if …

Part 2 An essay

Your teacher has asked you to write an essay on the following statement: 'Children spend too much time watching television.'

Write an essay of 120–180 words.

Nowadays many homes have more than one television, and some children even have a TV in their bedrooms. It is not surprising, then, that statistics show that watching television is the most popular leisure activity for the majority of children. (1)

There is no doubt that children need time to relax after school, and most children's programmes are certainly very entertaining. Furthermore, (2) some television programmes, especially documentaries and news programmes, are educational and informative, and can contribute to a child's education. (3) (4)

Having said that, (2) many children's programmes are of poor quality, and children learn nothing from them. What is more, (2) watching television is a very passive activity requiring no physical effort. In my view, it would be better if children spent more time on more creative and imaginative activities, and on sport. (3) (4)

To sum up, (2) I believe that parents should limit the amount of time that children spend in front of the television to one or two hours a day. Otherwise, we run the risk of creating generations of unhealthy and ill-educated young adults. (5)

1 Refer to the question in the first paragraph. Make a general statement about the question or briefly introduce arguments for and against.

2 Use linking words to connect ideas and sentences.

3 Present both sides of the argument, where appropriate giving examples that support the different points of view.

4 Put the two sides of the argument in separate paragraphs.

5 Express your own opinion in the final paragraph.

●●● Phrase Bank

Expressing your opinions
In my view/opinion, …
I firmly believe that …
It seems to me that …

Expressing other people's views
Some people think/claim/believe that …
It is sometimes said that …
It could be argued that …

Making additional points
Furthermore, …
In addition, …
What is more, …

Expressing a contrast
While that may be true, …
On the other hand, …
However, …
Having said that, …

Summing up
To sum up, …
In conclusion, …
On balance, I feel that …

Part 2 A story

Write a story beginning with these words:

Simon woke up suddenly. What was that noise he had just heard?

Write 120–180 words.

Simon woke up (5) suddenly. What was that noise he had just heard (5)? He listened carefully (3). After a while, (2) he heard the noise again. It sounded like there was someone downstairs in the kitchen! (1) (6)

He wasn't sure what to do, so first, (2) he looked around for some sort of weapon, and found his tennis racket. Then (2) he went quietly (3) out onto the landing and looked down the stairs. He couldn't see anything, so he crept slowly (3) down the stairs, stopping (5) every so often to listen again. Suddenly, there was a crashing (3) sound. 'What on earth was that?' (4) he thought worriedly. (1) (6)

He started to run down the stairs. Meanwhile, (2) the crashing started again. He threw open the kitchen door and shouted, 'Stop!'. (4) Nobody was there. But there was that terrible (3) noise again! (6) Eventually, (2) he opened a cupboard and out jumped the cat! It had got shut inside, and had been knocking over (5) packets and tins of food trying to get out. 'Silly cat!' (4) said Simon, feeling very relieved. (1)

1 Give your story a clear beginning, middle and end.

2 Use sequencing words to order the events.

3 Use adjectives and adverbs to make your writing more lively and interesting.

4 Try to use some direct and/or indirect speech.

5 Use a variety of narrative tenses.

6 Creating atmosphere and suspense will make your story more enjoyable.

●●● **Phrase Bank**

Ordering events
As soon as …
While …
By the time …
First, …
Next, …
Then, …
After a while, …
Meanwhile, …
Suddenly, …
Eventually …

Grammar Reference

Articles

We use the indefinite article *a/an*

1 when we say what something is or what it is like:
What's that? It's a radio.
My sister drives an expensive German car.

2 when we say what somebody's job is:
Tom Cruise is a film actor.

3 when we describe somebody's features:
He's got a long face and a small moustache.

We use *the*

1 when it's clear what we are talking about. This can be because we've already mentioned it:
I've got a cat and a dog. The dog is called Rover.

or because there is only one:
You shouldn't look directly at the sun.

or because it's clear from the situation:
Could you pass me the dictionary? (The one that's on the table over there.)

2 with most nationality words:
The English have a reputation for being bad cooks.

3 with the names of rivers, mountain ranges, deserts and seas:
the Nile, the Himalayas, the Sahara, the Mediterranean

4 with a few countries and most groups of islands:
the United States   the Netherlands   the Czech Republic
the Canaries   the Seychelles   the Maldives

5 in various set phrases, for example:
go to the cinema   listen to the radio
play the piano/the guitar, etc.
in the morning/the afternoon/the evening

We don't use an article

1 when we are making generalisations:
Cats chase mice.

2 with most countries, continents, towns and cities, lakes and mountains:
Mount Everest is in Asia, on the border between Nepal and Tibet.

3 with some nouns following a preposition:
go to work/school   be in bed/hospital/prison

4 with meals:
have breakfast/lunch/dinner

Simple and continuous tenses

Overview

1 We generally use continuous tenses to describe temporary situations:
It's snowing.
I've been getting a lot of headaches recently.
We generally use simple tenses to state facts:
It snows a lot in Finland.
I've never had toothache.

2 We generally use simple tenses for very short actions or events:
The bomb exploded.
We generally use continuous tenses for things happening over a longer time:
We noticed that the boat was sinking.

3 We often use continuous tenses to talk about duration (how long):
She has been directing films since the age of twenty.
We never use continuous tenses to say how many times something happens, will happen, has happened, etc:
By the end of this year, she will have made twelve films.

4 Continuous tenses are normally used for actions or events, rather than states:
Please be quiet, I'm reading. (action)
We normally use simple tenses for states:
These books belong to the library. (state)

Non-continuous verbs

Some verbs are not used in continuous tenses. These include:

1 mental states
 believe doubt hate know like love
 prefer realise recognise regret remember
 suppose understand want

2 communication
 agree disagree mean

3 other verbs
 belong contain cost depend fit matter
 need owe own possess seem

Some verbs are non-continuous with some meanings but not with others. For example, *think* is not used in continuous tenses when it means 'have an opinion':

 *I **think** reality TV shows are boring.*

 BUT *I'm **thinking** about my last holiday.*

Non-continuous	Continuous
I feel I should tell her the truth. (believe)	I'm feeling unwell.
My cousin has a Porsche. (possess)	Where are we having lunch?
Does this fish taste funny? (have a flavour)	He burnt his mouth while he was tasting the soup.
I don't see the point of this. (understand)	We're seeing the doctor at 1.00.
Do you consider yourself an adult? (believe)	The council is considering closing the leisure centre.
I imagine we'll eat out. (think)	He was imagining what it would be like to be rich.
The shop appears to be closed. (seem)	Kevin Spacey is appearing on stage in London next week.

Present tenses

The present simple

We use the present simple

1 to talk about a habitual or repeated action or event:
 My grandfather runs 3km every morning.

2 to state a general fact:
 Koala bears sleep more than 20 hours a day.

3 for actions and events in a story, especially when describing the plot of a book, film, etc:
 Scout goes to school for the first time that autumn and has a terrible day.

4 with verbs not used in continuous tenses (see non-continuous verbs in previous column).

5 to refer to a future action or event that is part of a timetable:
 The next train to Manchester leaves in ten minutes.

The present continuous

We use the present continuous

1 to talk about an action or event that is in progress now:
 Put the umbrella up, it's raining.

2 to talk about an action or event which is repeated, but only around this time:
 I'm drinking too much coffee these days.

3 to talk about a temporary situation:
 My brother's working in China. (He normally works in France.)

4 to talk about changes in a situation:
 Air travel is getting cheaper.

5 (with always) to complain about annoying behaviour:
 That dog is always jumping on the sofa.

6 to refer to a future action or event that has been arranged:
 Which country is hosting the next Olympics?

Talking about the future

will and *going to*

We use *will*

1 to make impersonal, factual statements about the future:
Work on the new stadium will begin next year.

2 to make predictions based on your own beliefs:
I'm sure you'll enjoy the play.
NB We often use will after phrases like:
I think, I don't think, I imagine, I reckon, I'm certain

3 when you make an instant decision about what to do next:
That soup smells delicious. I'll try some.

4 to talk about future events that are dependent on other events:
If we leave now, we'll be home before nightfall.

5 to make offers and promises:
Don't worry, I won't tell anyone your secret.

6 to add a question tag to an imperative or make a tag reply:
Don't tell anyone, will you?
'Don't forget your passport.' 'I won't.'

We use *going to*

1 to talk about things you have decided to do:
I'm going to apply for a better job.

NB We usually avoid using *going to* with the verb *go*; we can use the present continuous instead.
I'm going to the theatre tomorrow.

2 to make predictions based on what is happening now.
It looks like this match is going to be a draw.

The present simple

We use the present simple with a future meaning

1 to talk about things that are due to happen as part of a schedule:
The next train to Manchester leaves in half an hour.

2 after certain words and phrases, for example:
when, as soon as, by the time, the moment, provided, assuming, if:
I'll give Jason his present as soon as he arrives.

The present continuous

We use the present continuous with a future meaning to talk about arrangements that we have made for the future, usually with other people:
I can't go out tomorrow night. I'm having dinner with my grandparents.

The future continuous

We use the future continuous

1 to talk about an action that will be in progress at a specific point in the future:
At midday tomorrow, I'll be taking my exams.

2 to talk about planned events. Used like this, it is similar to the present continuous for arrangements:
Next year, I'll be spending most of the summer abroad.

3 to ask polite and less direct questions about somebody's plans:
Will you be staying at the hotel for two nights or three?

The future perfect simple

We use the future perfect simple to talk about a completed action or event in the future:
By the time they get home, they'll have travelled more than 10,000 km.

The future perfect continuous

We normally use the future perfect continuous to say how long an action or event will have been in progress at a specific point in the future:
By the time he takes part in the Olympics, he'll have been training for four years.

Review of past tenses

The past simple

We use the past simple

1   to talk about actions or events that happened at a particular time in the past:
    'I left work at 10.30.' Jackson replied. 'I took a taxi home.'

2   to describe a series of actions or events in the past:
    Jackson put on his coat, switched off the light, opened the door and walked out onto the street.

The past continuous

We use the past continuous

1   to describe a scene in the past:
    It was 2 a.m. but the city wasn't sleeping. Music was coming from countless upstairs windows.

2   to talk about actions or events that were in progress around a particular time in the past:
    'What were you doing at 11 o'clock yesterday evening?' asked the policeman.

3   We often use the past simple and the past continuous together to describe how one event interrupted another, longer event:
    While Jackson was looking for the right address, a police car came around the corner.

The present perfect simple

We use the present perfect simple

1   to talk about recent events, particularly when giving news:
    Have you heard? Tom and Nancy have just got married!

    NB We often use the present perfect simple for events within a period of time that continues up to the present moment. Words which often go with the present perfect simple include: *ever, never, just, already, yet,* and *so far.*

2   to talk about an event that began in the past and continues up to the present, particularly with non-continuous verbs:
    I've had this skateboard since I was six years old.

    NB With verbs which can be used in continuous tenses, we normally use the present perfect continuous, not simple, to say how long an action has been in progress: *'I've been waiting for hours!'*

3   to talk about recent past events that have a result in the present:
    You've broken my laptop. Now I can't check my emails.

4   to talk about experiences at an unstated time in the past:
    Have you ever been to Rome? I've never tried rock-climbing.

The present perfect continuous

We use the present perfect continuous

1   to talk about recent actions or events that are not necessarily complete:
    You've been spending too much money recently. (And you might continue to spend too much.)

    NB *When the action is complete, we use the present perfect simple. Compare: I've been writing a novel. I'm on chapter 4./I've written a novel. It was published last year.*

2   to say how long an action or event has been in progress:
    I've been learning the guitar for six years.

3   to explain a current situation in terms of recent events:
    My trousers are muddy because I've been planting trees in the garden.

The past perfect simple

We use the past perfect simple to talk about an event that happened before another event in the past:
    I wanted some pasta, but my brother had eaten it all.

The past perfect continuous

The two most common uses of the past perfect continuous are

1   for saying how long an action had been in progress up to a certain point in the past:
    By the age of 18, my grandfather had been working in a factory for six years.

2   to explain a past situation in terms of previous events:
    Terry was upset because his sister had been making fun of him.

used to

We use *used to*

1 to describe habits in the past:
   I used to go skating every weekend.

2 to describe a situation in the past that is different now:
   There didn't use to be any shops in this part of town. (But there are now.)

would

We sometimes use *would* to describe habits in the past, especially in literary texts.

Every evening, the princess would gaze out of the window longingly.

NB We can't use *would* to talk about situations in the past:

When I was younger I ~~would be~~ afraid of the dark. (… I used to be afraid …)

Verb patterns

verb + *–ing* or infinitive

When we put two verbs together, the second verb is usually in the infinitive or *–ing* form. Which pattern we use depends on the first verb.

verb + infinitive	verb + –ing form	Verb + infinitive or –ing form (same meaning)
agree	avoid	begin
dare	can't face	continue
decide	can't help	hate
expect	can't stand	like
fail	don't mind	love
happen	enjoy	prefer
hope	fancy	start
manage	feel like	
mean	finish	
offer	give up	
prepare	imagine	
pretend	keep	
promise	postpone	
refuse	practise	
seem	put off	
want	recommend	
	risk	
	spend time	
	suggest	

A few verbs can take an infinitive or *–ing form* but the meaning is different:

1 a) If you **try doing** something, you do it in order to see what happens.
      He tried ringing the bell, but there was no answer.

  b) If you **try to do** something, you attempt it but do not necessarily achieve it.
      He tried to reach the next branch, but it was too high.

2 a) If you **stop doing** something, you do not do it any longer.
      They stopped talking when I walked into the room.

  b) If you **stop to do** something, you come to a halt in order to do something.
      She stopped to admire the flowers.

3 a) If you **remember doing** something, you have an image of doing it in your mind.
      I remember going to the circus when I was a child.

  b) If you **remember to do** something, you do something which is on your mental list of things to do.
      Did you remember to feed the fish?

4 a) If you **go on doing** something, you continue doing it.
      He went on talking for hours.

  b) If you go on to do something, you move from one action to another.
      The chairman welcomed the audience, then he went on to introduce the guest speakers.

see (*watch, hear, feel, etc.*) somebody do/doing something

1 We can use *see* (*watch, hear, feel,* etc.) + object + *–ing* form to talk about an action that is progress.
   She saw two men crossing the river. (They were in the water when she saw them.)

2 We can use *see* (*watch, hear, feel,* etc.) + object + infinitive without *to* to talk about an action that is complete.
   She saw two men cross the river. (She watched them cross from one side to the other.)

Reported speech

Tense changes

1   When we report somebody's words rather than quoting them directly, we usually change the tense of any verbs:

'It's late,' he said.   *He said that it was late.*

NB We often omit the word *that* from the beginning of the reported speech clause:

He said it was late.

The normal pattern of tense changes in reported speech is:

Direct speech	Reported speech
present simple	past simple
present continuous	past continuous
past simple	past perfect simple
present perfect simple	past perfect simple
present perfect continuous	past perfect continuous
past continuous	past perfect continuous
will	*would*
shall	*should*
may/might	*might*
must	*must/had to*
can	*could*

2   There are often changes in words which refer to the people, time or place. These are dictated more by logic than by any rules:

'I'm bringing my brother here tomorrow,' she said.
She said that she was taking her brother there the next day.

say and tell

1   The object of the verb *say* is always what was said. It is often a clause:

She said she would like to go to university.

If we want to mention the person who is addressed, we must use the preposition *to*:

Would you like to say hello to my cousin?
'You're lucky,' she said to her friend.

2   The object of the verb *tell* is usually the person who is addressed. We do not use the preposition *to*:

Have you told your parents?
They told me the shop was closed.

We also use *tell* in set phrases like *tell a lie, tell the truth, tell a story*, etc.

Reported questions

1   When we report questions, we use affirmative word order and verb forms after the question word:

'Where do you live?' she asked him.
She asked him where he lived.

2   To report a yes/no question (one that has no question word) we use *whether* or *if*:

'Is it raining?' he asked.
He asked if/whether it was raining.

3   We can sometimes use an infinitive in a reported question, especially when it's a question about our own actions:

'Which shirt shall I wear?' he asked his girlfriend.
He asked his girlfriend which shirt to wear.

'How do I get to the beach?' she asked me.
She asked me how to get to the beach.

Infinitives in reported speech

1   We use the structure: reporting verb + object + infinitive to report imperatives. Some common reporting verbs for this structure are *tell, order, instruct, warn, ask* and *beg*:

'Don't be late,' the teacher told him.
The teacher told him not to be late.

'Please help me,' he said to his friend.
He asked his friend to help him.

NB We cannot use this structure with the reporting verb say:

We ~~said to him~~ to be careful. (We told him ...)

We can use the same structure for reporting advice:

'I think you should go to bed,' Mary said to her son.
Mary advised her son to go to bed.

2   We can use the structure: reporting verb + infinitive with *agree, promise* and *offer*. (Note that we cannot include an object.)

'I'll remember you forever,' he said to her.
He promised to remember her forever.

3   See above for infinitives in reported questions.

Modals

Advice, obligation and prohibition

We use *should (shouldn't)* and *ought to (ought not to)*

1 for giving advice:
I think you should stay at home this evening.

2 for giving opinions about what the right thing to do is:
We all ought to use less electricity.

NB In the negative, it is more natural to say *'I don't think you should …'* than *'I think you shouldn't …'*.

We use *must*

1 for giving strong advice to ourselves:
I must try to get to bed early tonight.

2 for making strong recommendations to others, based on our own opinions:
You must try this cake, it's wonderful.

3 for stating rules, especially in written and formal English:
Cyclists must wear helmets.

We use *have to* to talk about obligation:
We have to sit exams every year. (They're compulsory.)

NB We use *I have to…* for things that we are obliged to do; we use *I must…* for things that we strongly feel we should do. Compare: *I must start cycling to work. It would be good exercise./I have to start cycling to work. They've cancelled the only bus.*

We use *don't/doesn't have to* for things that we do not need to do. It expresses a lack of obligation; it does not express prohibition:
You don't have to leave now. You can stay as long as you like.

We use *mustn't* for prohibition:
You mustn't touch the walls. The paint isn't dry.

NB Except for the specific uses mentioned here, *must* and *mustn't* can often sound unnatural; we are more likely to use other verbs and phrases for talking about obligation (*have to*) and prohibition (*against the rules, forbidden, not allowed*, etc.)

Ability

1 We use *can* for talking about ability in the present:
Can you see that man on the roof?
Speak up, I can't hear you.

2 *Can* sometimes refers to a future event, but only when the decision is being made in the present:
'Can you come to dinner next week?' 'No, but I can make the week after.'

However, we normally *will be able to* when we talk about ability in the future:
When she's 17, she'll be able to take her driving test.

3 We use *could/couldn't* to talk about general ability in the past:
My grandfather could speak three languages fluently.

However, we do not use *could* (affirmative form) to talk about something we were able to do on one occasion. We use an alternative expression like *managed to do* or *succeed in doing*:
It was a difficult question, but I managed to answer it.

4 We often use *can* and *could* with verbs of perception like *see, taste* and *hear*. (We can use *could* even when it's one occasion.)
Pressing my ear to the door, I could hear what they were saying.

Permission and requests

1 We often use *can/can't* when we ask for, give or refuse permission:
Can I borrow your pen?   Yes, of course.
You can sit anywhere you like.

Could I …? and *May I …?* are slightly politer ways of requesting permission:
Could/May I sit next to you?   Yes, you may.

NB We don't normally use 'Yes, you could' or 'No, you couldn't' as replies to a request for permission, even if the request uses *could*.

An even politer form is *Would you mind if I … (+ past simple)?*
Would you mind if I opened a window?

2 We often use *Can you …?* to ask somebody to do something:
Can you explain that again, please?

Could you …? , *Would you …?* and *Would you mind (+ –ing)* are all slightly politer ways of asking somebody to do something:
Would you mind opening the window?

Speculating

1 We use *must* for talking about things which we can deduce are definitely true:
   He must be tired. He's just run 10 km.

2 We use *may* or *might* for speculating about things that are possibly true. (Some people use *might* when there is less possibility.) We can also use *could* to talk about possibility. However, we cannot use the negative *(couldn't)* in this sense:
   Geoff isn't answering his phone at work. He might not be at his desk. He could be in a meeting, or he may be having lunch.

3 We use *can't* for talking about things which we can deduce are impossible:
   This can't be Suzie's jacket. It's much too small.

4 When we are making logical deductions about something in the past, we use *must have* and *can't have* + past participle:
   I put odd socks on this morning. I must have been half asleep.
   Your parents can't have been very happy when you told them you were dropping out of university.

5 When we are speculating about something in the past, we use *may have*, *might have*, or *could have* + past participle:
   Police think the robbers may have used a white van as their escape vehicle.

   We cannot use *may have* for things which we now know didn't happen. We use *might have* or *could have*:
   That was a dangerous thing to do. You might have been injured.

Passives

Use

We use the passive

1 when we don't know who or what is responsible for the action:
   My bike was stolen last week.

2 for stylistic reasons, especially to allow the main focus of the sentence to be the subject of the verb:
   The saxophone is quite a modern instrument. <u>It was invented around 1840 by Adolphe Sax</u> and has since become an essential part of jazz and popular music.

Tenses

The tense of a passive construction is determined by the tense of the verb be:
   Most children's toys are made in China (present simple)
   This shirt was bought in Italy. (past simple)
   By August, the roof had been repaired but the windows were still being replaced. (past perfect, past continuous)
   The film will be shown at cinemas next month. (future simple)

Verbs with two objects

1 With verbs that often have two objects (*give, offer, owe, award, tell, send, teach*, etc.) either object can become the subject of a passive sentence:
   Jack was given the prize for best costume.
   The prize for best costume was given to Jack.

   NB It is more common for the indirect object (usually a person) to be the subject of the passive sentence.

2 If we include an agent, we usually put it at the end of the sentence:
   She was offered a new job in the company <u>by her boss</u>.

Passive with *know, believe, think,* etc.

1 Verbs like *know, believe* and *think* are often used in passive constructions, especially in formal language, and are followed by an infinitive:
   At that time, the world was thought to be flat.

2 If the sentence refers to a current belief about a past event, we use the present simple passive followed by a perfect infinitive *(to have done something)*:
   Beethoven is now known to have suffered from lead poisoning. (But that wasn't known at the time.)

3 We can also use an impersonal construction with *it* + passive:
   At that time, it was thought that the world was flat.
   It is now known that Beethoven suffered from lead poisoning.

Passive infinitive and *-ing* form

1 We can use passive infinitives – *(to) be done, (to) have been done* – in a similar way to other infinitives, for example, as part of a verb pattern or after most modal verbs:
This watch can be worn underwater.
Mobile phones must not be used on flights.
Some passengers pretended to have been injured in order to claim insurance.

2 We can use passive *-ing* forms – *being done, having been done* – in a similar way to other *-ing* forms:
Many celebrities do not enjoy being photographed.
She denied having been given the documents.
Having been identified by witnesses, the suspect was arrested and charged.

so and *such*

1 We use *so* and *such* for emphasis. They make the meaning of an adjective, adverb or noun stronger.

2 We use *so* before an adjective (without a noun) or an adverb:
I'm so hungry!   *Why are you talking so quickly?*

3 We use *such* before a noun or before an adjective + noun. Note that the indefinite article (*a/an*), if needed, comes after the word such:
That's such a lie!   *Why are dogs such faithful pets?*
You're such a good swimmer.

4 We often use *so* with quantifiers like *much, many, few* and *little*. However, we say *such a lot (of …)*:
I've never seen so many insects!   *There's so much to do and so little time.*
We've got such a lot of homework.

5 We often use *so* and *such* followed by a relative clause to express a result:
The exam was so difficult that only three students passed.
(OR *It was such a difficult exam that only three students passed.*)
She spoke so quietly that nobody heard.

Relative clauses
Relative pronouns

1 Relative clauses usually begin with a relative pronoun (*who, which, that, whose*) or a relative adverb (*when, where*).

2 The relative pronoun *whom* can be used instead of *who* when it is the object of the verb in the relative clause. However, for many speakers of English, *whom* sounds very formal and *who* is preferred:
The former headmaster, whom many parents disliked, resigned last year.

We also use *whom* immediately after a preposition; we cannot use *who* in this context unless we move the preposition to the end of the clause:
She married the man with whom she'd shared an office.
She married the man (who) she'd shared an office with.

3 Defining relative clauses can also begin with *what*, meaning 'the thing which'.
I did exactly what you asked.

Defining relative clauses

1 A defining relative clause comes after a noun and gives necessary information about that noun. It can be in the middle or at the end of a sentence and is not normally separated by commas:
Did you get the job that you applied for?
The factory where my dad works is closing down.

2 It is more common to use *that* than *which* in defining relative clauses, especially in spoken English. We can also use *that* instead of *who* or *whom*:
I'd love to meet the person that wrote this song.

3 We can sometimes omit the relative pronoun in a defining relative clause, but only when it is the object of the verb in the clause:
Where's the pen (that) I bought this morning? (We can omit *that*.)

BUT *I'm looking for a shop that sells skateboards.* (We cannot omit *that*.)

We often omit the relative adverb *when*:
I still remember the moment (when) I first saw Juliet.

Non-defining relative clauses

1 A non-defining relative clause comes after a noun and gives extra information about that noun. A non-defining relative clause can be removed from a sentence without making the sentence meaningless. It can be in the middle or at the end of a sentence and is separated by commas:
We spent a few days in Windhoek, which is the capital of Namibia.
Our neighbour, who used to be an actor, has started a drama society.

2 A non-defining relative clause cannot start with *that.*

3 The relative pronoun or adverb at the start of a non-defining relative clause cannot be omitted.

4 Non-defining relative clauses can begin with expressions like *all of whom, many of whom, some of whom, most of which,* etc:
The company employs more than 3,000 staff, many of whom are women.

5 Sometimes, the relative pronoun *which* can be used at the start of a non-defining relative clause to refer back to all the information in the first part of the sentence, rather than just the noun before it:
I managed to visit six different countries, which was amazing.

Reduced relative clauses

1 A reduced relative clause replaces a defining relative clause. We use an *–ing* form or a past participle to replace the relative pronoun and verb.

2 We use an *–ing* form to replace an active verb of any tense; we use a past participle to replace a passive verb of any tense:
She wears a necklace originally belonging to her grandmother. (= which originally belonged to ...)
The president visited several towns damaged by the flood. (= which were damaged)

3 We can't use a reduced relative clause in place of a defining relative clause if the relative pronoun is the object of the verb in the original clause:
She wears a necklace that she made herself. (cannot be reduced)

Comparatives and superlatives

Short adjectives

1 In the context of forming comparatives and superlatives, short adjectives are
* most adjectives with one syllable, but not past participles like *bored* or *scared.*
* two-syllable adjectives which end in *–y, –le, –er* or *–ow* (e.g. *ugly, little, clever, shallow*)

2 We add *–er* to short adjectives to make the comparative form, and *–est* to make the superlative form:
long – longer – longest
If the adjective ends in *–e*, we add *–r* or *–st*:
wide – wider – widest

If the adjective ends in a single vowel and consonant, we double the consonant and add *–er*, or *–est*:
hot – hotter – hottest

If the adjective ends *–y*, we change the *–y* into *–ier*, or *–iest*:
friendly – friendlier – friendliest

3 Some adjectives have irregular comparative and superlative forms:
good – better –best
bad – worse – worst
far – further – furthest

We can use *elder* and *eldest* instead of *older* and *oldest*, but only when we talk about people (and usually in relation to brothers and sisters).

Long adjectives

We use *more* and *most* for most long adjectives (adjectives with more than one syllable):
exciting – more exciting – most exciting

Adverbs

1 We add *more* and *most* to adverbs to form the comparative and superlative. (Even though we add –*er* and –*est* to two-syllable adjectives ending in –*ly*, we use *more* and *most* for two-syllable adverbs.)
clearly   more clearly   most clearly

2 Some irregular adverbs have comparative and superlative forms ending –*er* and –*est*, as do adverbs which share the same form as a short adjective (e.g. *fast, early, late, hard*):
well – better – best
badly – worse – worst
fast – faster – fastest

than in comparisons

We use *than* when we make a comparison. It can be followed by a noun or a clause:
Steve Martin is funnier than Jim Carrey.
That meal was nicer than I thought it was going to be.

in with superlatives

A superlative is often followed by *in* when we define the group:
She's the most successful student in the school.
It's the most poisonous plant in the world.

more and *most*, *less* and *least*

1 We use *more* and *most* as comparative and superlative forms of *much/many*:
I ate more than my brother, but my dad ate the most.
There were more people at the meeting than last year.

2 We can also use *more* and *most* to mean 'to a greater (or the greatest) extent':
Consumers are starting to complain more.
Which pattern do you like most?

3 *Less* and *least* have the opposite meaning to *more* and *most*:
I'm trying to eat less.
What do you like least about your town?

4 We can also use *less* and *least* with adjectives (short and long) or adverbs:
We're less poor than we used to be.
Which actor performed least well, in your opinion?

(not) as … as

1 We can use *as … as* or *just as … as* to say that two people or things are the same:
I'm as scared as you are!
Aaron sings just as beautifully as his brother.

2 We use *not as … as* to mean *less … than*:
Cycling isn't as tiring as running. = *Cycling is less tiring than running.*

Subject and object pronouns

When using a personal pronoun in the second part of a comparison, we normally use the object pronoun. The subject pronoun sounds very formal unless it's followed by a verb:
You're stronger than me. (✓)
She's taller than I. (very formal/archaic)
He isn't as intelligent as I am. (✓)

Other comparative and superlative expressions

1 To intensify the meaning of a comparative, we can use *much* or *far* (but not *very*):
That film was much/far better than I expected.

We can use *by far* with superlatives:
This is by far the worst hotel I've ever stayed in.

2 Other common expressions that use comparative and superlative forms include:
The more you exercise, the healthier you'll feel.
Computers are getting more and more powerful, but less and less easy to understand.
The simplest things in life are often the most enjoyable.

Conditionals

General rules

1. All conditional sentences have an *if* clause (a condition) and a main clause (a result). In general terms, the main clause says what happens as a result of the *if* clause being true:

   If it rains tomorrow, we'll stay at home.
   (condition)   (result)

2. We can put either clause first in the sentence. When the *if* clause is first, it is usually followed by a comma. When the main clause is first, there is usually no comma:

   I'd fix your phone if I knew how.

Type 0 conditionals

1. We use a type 0 conditional to talk about a result which always follows from a particular action. We use the present simple to talk about both the action and its result:

   If you don't water indoor plants, they die.

2. We can also use a type 0 conditional to give orders and advice, using an imperative in the main clause:

   If you want to know the answer, turn to the back of the book.

Type 1 conditionals

1. We use a type 1 conditional to talk about a future action, event or situation and its result:

   If you're late, I'll be very angry.
   (condition)   (result)

   NB This is the only type of conditional which always refers to the future.

2. We use the present simple in the *if* clause and the future simple (with *will*) in the main clause.

3. We only use a type 1 conditional when the condition is possible. If it is not, we use a type 2 conditional.

Type 2 conditionals

1. We use a type 2 conditional to talk about a hypothetical action, event or situation and its (hypothetical) result:

   If I were taller, I'd be better at basketball.

2. A type 2 conditional can refer to the present or future. When it refers to the future, it differs from a type 1 conditional in that the condition is much less likely to come true:

   Would you share the money with me if you won the lottery?
         (result)   (condition)

3. We normally use the past simple in the *if* clause and *would* in the main clause. The past tense expresses the fact that it is a hypothetical situation – it does not refer to the past.

   I wouldn't be so upset if you weren't my best friend.

   We occasionally use the past continuous instead of the past simple:

   If they were playing better, they'd have more chance of winning.

4. In the *if* clause, we often use *were* instead of *was*, particularly with the first person, *I*:

   If I was/were you, I'd tell her how you feel.

Type 3 conditionals

1. Like type 2 conditionals, type 3 conditionals refer to hypothetical situations. However, type 3 conditionals are the only type which refer to the past. They are used to speculate about how things might have been different:

   If you had revised, you wouldn't have failed your exam.

2. We use the past perfect (*had/hadn't done*) in the *if* clause and *would/wouldn't have* in the main clause:

   I wouldn't have told him if I'd known it was a secret.

   NB *Would* and *had* can both appear as the short form *'d*. *Would* is always in the main clause, *had* in the *if* clause.

3. We can also use the past perfect continuous in the *if* clause:

   If you'd been watching the road, you wouldn't have crashed.

Mixed conditionals

Mixed conditionals are usually a mixture of types 2 and 3 and refer to hypothetical situations. Mixed conditionals occur when the time reference in the *if* clause is different from the main clause:

If I had gone to bed earlier,	past (type 3)
I wouldn't be so tired today.	present (type 2)
If I were your father,	present (type 2)
I wouldn't have let you stay out all night.	past (type 3)

If I weren't going away tomorrow,	future (type 2)
I'd have accepted your invitation.	past (type 3)
If she hadn't spent all her money,	past (type 3)
she'd get a taxi home.	future (type 2)

Causatives

have, make, let and *get*

1 We use the structure *to have something done* to talk about things which we do not do ourselves but instead, pay or ask somebody else to do:
   Have you had your hair cut?
   They've had their house decorated.

2 We can use *to get something done* in the same way. The meaning is the same:
   I'd need to get my car repaired.

3 We sometimes use *to have* (or *get*) something done to talk about unpleasant things which happen to us as a result of somebody else's actions:
   He had his bike stolen.
   Be careful. You might get your fingers burnt!

4 We use the structure *to make somebody do something* to talk about things we cause or force somebody to do:
   This film really makes me laugh.
   His parents made him clean his room.

5 We also use *make* in the passive to talk about things we are caused or forced to do. However, we use an infinitive with *to*, rather than a bare infinitive, after the passive. Compare:
   They made the hostages lie on the floor.
   The hostages were made to lie on the floor.

6 We use the structure *to let somebody do something* to talk about things we allow somebody to do:
   She never lets her husband drive.

to want/need something done

We use the structure to *want/prefer/need something done* to talk about actions that we want or need somebody else to do:
   I need this jacket dry-cleaned by tomorrow.
   Would you like your fish grilled or fried?

OXFORD
UNIVERSITY PRESS

Great Clarendon Street, Oxford OX2 6DP

Oxford University Press is a department of the University of Oxford.
It furthers the University's objective of excellence in research, scholarship,
and education by publishing worldwide in

Oxford New York

Auckland Cape Town Dar es Salaam Hong Kong Karachi
Kuala Lumpur Madrid Melbourne Mexico City Nairobi
New Delhi Shanghai Taipei Toronto

With offices in

Argentina Austria Brazil Chile Czech Republic France Greece
Guatemala Hungary Italy Japan Poland Portugal Singapore
South Korea Switzerland Thailand Turkey Ukraine Vietnam

OXFORD and OXFORD ENGLISH are registered trade marks of
Oxford University Press in the UK and in certain other countries

ISBN: 978 0 19 480027 3

Printed in Spain by Orymu, S.A.

ACKNOWLEDGEMENTS

*The authors and publisher are grateful to those who have given permission to reproduce
the following extracts and adaptations of copyright material:* p38 *It's all been fun and
laughter for giggling girls and grunting guys* from *New Scientist*, issue 29 September
2001 © New Scientist. Reproduced by permission. p46 *When the music takes
you* from *New Scientist*, issue 29 October 2005 © New Scientist. Reproduced by
permission.

Sources: www.sciencedaily.com/releases; www.guardian.co.uk/france;
www.telegraph.co.uk

*Although every effort has been made to trace and contact copyright holders before
publication, this has not been possible in come cases. We apologize for any infringement
of copyright and if notified, the publisher will be pleased to rectify any errors or
omissions at the earliest opportunity.*

We would like to thank the following for their permission to reproduce photographs:
Cover photograph: courtesy Getty Images/George Doyle/Stockbyte. 4Corners
Images pp18 (cyclists/Fiore Daniele), 24 (1/Giovanni Simeone), 27 (2/Stanciu),
69 (cruise ship/Günter Gräfenhain, horse riding/Riccardo Spila) 93 (5/Massimo
Pignatelli), 99 (1/Giovanni Simeone), 127 (girls/Massimo Borchi); Alamy p84
(Ashley Cooper), p114 (surfing/Chris George), p115 (wind-surfing/Leo Mason);
Holly Allen p71; Alpha p9 (4); Arena p38 (Marilyn Kingwill); Aurora p11
(boys/Marnie Crawford Samuelson/IPN); Axiom p99 (2/Naki Kouyioumtzis);
Bridgeman p53 (*Flying Machines*, pen & ink on paper, © Bibliotheque de
l'Institut de France, Paris/Alinari); Camera Press, London pp18 (girls and
rucksacks/Eberhard Grames/Bilderberg), 19 (girls shopping/Dominic Asbach/
Bilderberg), 75 (4/Fechner/Laif, 5/Emmler/Laif), 99 (4/Knechtel/Laif) 107
(Kanchana Ketkeaw, scorpion/Cedric Arnold), 142 (PEROU); Cephas pp93 (3/
Fresh Food Images), 99 (3/Tim Hill); Corbis pp26 (landscape/George H.H.Huey),
27 (1/Bob Krist), 42 (guide dog/Jim Craigmyle), 45 (dancer/Peter Poby/Zefa),
68 (Bettmann), 69 (plane/Gerolf Kalt/Zefa), 81 (1/Hans Neleman/Zefa), 88
(mail symbol/Gregor Schuster/Zefa), 105 (1/Rainer Holz/Zefa), 107 (Lynne
Cox/Outline/Patrik Giardino), 108 (H.R.Bowers/Bettmann), 109 (Bettmann),
121 (3/lobster/ Klaus Hackenberg/Zefa), 123 (2/Henry Watkins & Yibran
Aragon/Reuters), 137 (IngoWagner/epa/Corbis),154 (4/Richard Ross);
Eyevine pp22 (2/Heidi and Hans-Juergen Koch), 23 (Ivan Mishokov/Jeremy Nicholl),
45 (film director/Jim Ruymen/United Press International), 94 (dish/Jiri Rezac),
99 (3/Mark Peterson/Redux, 5/TCS) 113 (2/Ed Alcock), 134 (3/Todd Rosenberg/

Polaris); Fat Duck p95; Getty pp9 (2/Hal Horowitz), 10-11 (girls/Howard
Kinsnorth), 23 (Ramu/Hulton Archive), 45 (inventor/scientist/Sean Justice),
69 (scooter/Volo Pictures), 81 (2/Scott Barbour, 4/Beth Dixson), 87 (1/David
Noton, 3/Bruce Laurance), 96 (2/Trish Gant, 4/Richard Sprang, 5/Ian O'Leary,
7/Dorling Kindersley), 105 (2/Richard Kolker, 3/Rachel Watson), 117 (2/Willie
Maldonado, 3/Bruce Laurance, 4/Stevenvotecotcom, 5/Martin Barraud,
6/LWA), 121 (2/city/Scott Warren), 123 (1/Noah Clayton), 125 (1/Laureen
Middley, 2/Patrick Molnar), 129 (2/Veer.com, 5/Jeff Hunter); Hemis.fr p75 (3/
Ludovic Maisant); Imagestate pp21 (1), 24 (3,4), 87 (5), 93 (1,4/Foodfolio), 114
(climbing/Linda DeLay Joseph), 115 (hill-walking/Kevin Richardson), 129 (4);
Jupiter 19 (tennis/Elea Dumas), 21 (2), 29 (herd/Peter Charlesworth, bunch/
Greg Whitaker), 39 (clown), 40, 81 (5/Val Loh), 82-3 (TITUS), 87 (4/Timothy
Martin McGuire), 88 (computer/Glasshouse Images), 91 (Greg Friedler), 93 (2/
Ross Durant), 96 (6/Michael Pohuski), 97 (2/Claire Bock), (1/Benjamin Rondel
Photography), 139 (Jeff Corwin); David King p62; Kobal pp54 (Daniel Craig/
Casino Royale), 55 (MGM/United Artists/Sony), 65 (Walt Disney); Landmark
Media p51 (1/Paulo Pirez); London Features International p9 (7); Lonely Planet
pp24 (2/Dennis Johnson), 75 (1/Simon Foale); LookatSciences p134 (4/Hubert
Raguet); Magnum p21 (3/Ian Berry); Millennium Images 147 (1/Matthew
Somerjay); Minden Pictures pp24 (1/Frans Lanting), 29 (flock/Patricio Robles
Gil/Sierra Madre), 31 (Michael and Patricia Fogden), 147 (2/Mitsuaki Iwago);
MorgueFile p126 (newspaper); National Geographic p75 (2/James L.Stanfield);
NHPA pp23 (3/Daniel Heuclin), 23 (4/E.Hanumanta Rao), 80 Iain Green Nordic
Photos p82 (fire/Peo Quick); OUP pp12 (Hemera), 35 (Hemera), 117 (boy), 122
(dancer, beach, fast food), 127 (building inset); Oxfam p146 (3/Greg Williams);
PA Photos pp146 (2/Marco Ugarte/AP, 4/Antonio Calanni/AP), 149 (Daryl
Hannah/Dolores Ochoa/AP); Punchstock pp10 (young men), 39 (mime), 42
(pilot),121 (1/footballer), 125 (3,4); PYMCA pp87 (2/Catherine Booker), 97(3/
Eleanor Lindsay-Finn), 113 (1/Brian Sweeney), 114 (mountain-biking/STYLEY);
Retna pp9 (1/Starface, 6/Sara De Boer), 45 (singer-songwriter/JPI Studios);
Reuters pp28 Arnd Wiegmann, 69 (train), 129 (3/Kim Kyung Hoon); Rex
Features pp9 (3/Richard Young, 4/Action Press, 8/Everett Collection), 39 (The
Drowsy Chaperone/Alistair Muir), 46 (Andre Csillag), 47 (Huw John), 51(2/
ITV), 70 (Holly Allen), 94 (Dans le Noir exterior/Jonathan Hordle, Dans le Noir
entrance/Paul Cooper), 97 (1/Sipa Press), 119 (Nick Cunard), 143 (2/Sipa Press,
4/Jonathan Hordle), 146 (1/Sipa Press); Ronald Grant Archive pp14, 39 (His
New Job/RGA, Failure To Launch/Paramount Pictures), 48 (Universal Studios),
54 (Eva Green/Casino Royale, Mads Mikkelsen/Casino Royale, explosion/
Tomorrow Never Dies) EON, 54 (car chase), 58-9 (Dreamworks SKG), 64 (New
Line Cinema), 118 (United Artists), 134 (1, 2/Orion Pictures); Scala, Florence
pp52, 53 (architectural drawings); Science Photo Library p136 (Sam Ogden);
Still Pictures 151 (traffic/Henning Christoph/Das Fotoarchiv, rubbish/Martin
Bond); Superstock pp81 (3/Raymond Forbes), 96 (1/Mauritius), 151 (multi-
storey car-park/Age Fotostock); View Pictures 111 (1/Chris Gascoigne, 2/James
Brittain); WENN p143 (3).

Commissioned illustrations by: Billie Jean/ZeegenRush pp82, 103, 132, 135; Nigel
Paige pp34, 145.

Stock illustration by kind permission: Mr Bingo/ZeegenRush pp102 (vending
machine), 138; Jon Burgerman pp33, 110; Nishant Choksi p36; Brian
Grimwood p26; Adrian Johnson pp13, 67, 74, 100; Peter Mac pp73 (bus), 104,
116, 140; Joe Magee p66; Marine/ZeegenRush pp32, 37, 79, 124; Christian
Montenegro/Dutch Uncle p73 (star); Veronica Palmieri/Folio p60; Simon
Pemberton pp57, 130-1, 148-9, 150, 152; Pietari Posti/Debut Art p128;
Katherine Streeter/Dutch Uncle pp49, 76, 141; Neil Webb/Debut Art
pp15, 77, 92; Louise Weir pp16, 20, 41, 50, 61, 101.